Surprised
By
Grace

By
Noel Cromhout

xulon
PRESS

JUNE. 2012.

DEAR LA,

You ARE ONE OF GOD'S
VEHICLES OF GRACE TO US
ALL.

MAY YOU CONTINUE TO ENJOY
THIS AMAZING GRACE
DAY BY DAY.

GOD BLESS,

Noel Crowhurst.

DEDICATIONS

‹۞·۞›

M y thanks goes to family members and friends who have frequently encouraged me to write a book. Special thanks to son Stephen and his good wife Salome who recently gave me a strong push that finally got it going.

Daughter Delray, always enormously busy, somehow made time to proofread the script in its early stages.

I'm especially grateful to Angie Alvarez-Smith for lending her expertise and so much of her valuable time to proofread, edit and tidy up the script to make it acceptable for publishing. Thanks to her husband Michael also, for allowing his wife to get involved in such a time-consuming project!

My wife Merle is as always my greatest supporter. Above all, my thanks goes to my Lord and Savior Jesus Christ whose enabling grace constantly surprises and sustains me.

CONTENTS

CHAPTERS

Is this the story of my life? This little anecdote will answer that question.

An eager tourist, while visiting a historic village asked an elderly resident. "Have you lived here all your life?" The old feeler replied "Not yet!" Yes, I'm fairly "senior" in years, 70 something to be more specific. But, in the grace of God my life is not over, not yet! Neither is my usefulness to Him, and to His people. Caleb said, at age 85 "Now give me this mountain," and he took it from the giants that had put fear into the 10 Israeli spies 45 years previously!

I want to be like Caleb! Don't you?

So here goes with the story of my life. . . . .SO FAR!

CHAPTER 1
BEGINNINGS

—————⟶⟨⟩⟶—————

I am testimony to the truth of this passage in 1 Corinthians 1. "God has chosen the weak, foolish things of the world to confound the wise and powerful in the world." (PARAPHRASING VS 7-28) 2 Corinthians 12:9(b), where the Lord says, "My strength is made perfect in [your] weakness."

The fact that I have pastored 12 congregations in 43 years in the ministry, with a fair measure of success (only one of the twelve asked me to leave!) is testimony to the amazing enabling grace of the Lord.

I didn't finish high school. The only time I went to a Bible school is when I've been invited to preach there. The same is true with two universities. I was extremely shy and self-conscious. As an apprentice minister, I found it very difficult to visit church members and make new contacts. I was often intimidated by older men or women if, in my perception, they showed the slightest hint of hostility. I was a musician, and that's where I felt comfortable, seated at the keyboard and doing what I could do well, playing the piano.

So, you might ask, if that's how you felt as a young man, how come you became a trainee minister? Fair question! I'll try to give a simple answer, then an explanation. The simple answer: God called me. The explanation: As a young man my twin passions were the game of cricket, and music. After my conversion to Christ, I had a strong desire to please Him, and to make my life really count for Him.

CONSECRATION, in a movie house?

This desire reached a decisive point one night at the end of a Cecil B. DeMille movie I saw in the old 20th Century Fox cinema, a Bible epic entitled "The Robe." This movie depicted the courageous stand of some early Christians during the Roman persecution of the Early Church. I must inform you, this was not a Christian movie, it was a Hollywood presentation, and amplification of a man and woman, with a strong romantic flavor (of course!) who, for their bold stand for Christ, were executed together by Roman authorities. The movie was close enough to the Biblical account to have a profound effect on me that night. I vividly remember saying to the Lord as the houselights came on and the cinema audience began to head for the exits, "Lord, please do something useful with my life."

Soon after this I pulled out of the cocktail hour gigs and the dance band scene in which I played, and I was roped into playing piano for the meetings in the Assembly of God in East London, my hometown. I also arranged music and played for special choir items. I found that I was frequently sharing the Scriptures with choir members when I sensed they were having a spiritual struggle, and they seemed to be helped by what I shared. More by default than anything else, I became a sort of unofficial leader of the youth. There my ministry of the Word expanded, but still the major thrust was music, both in the local Assembly and with Youth For Christ (YFC).

Then, oh, horrors, people began to say. "When are you going into the ministry?" Be assured, I was not flattered, nor excited, I was disturbed! Music was my business, my very life, and I knew my way around the keyboard. But, I never entertained dreams of preaching to the masses, or even to just a few dozen! Full-time music ministry, yes! Preacher/Pastor . . . No! However, the Scriptures continued to come alive to me, and to my surprise I found a growing desire to preach the Word, and to help people apply what was preached to their lives.

I shared these thoughts with some of my local leaders. I was careful to say, "I'm not sure if this is the call of God, or if it is just my own desire to be in the ministry full time." I was wisely counseled, "Continue with what you're doing. If it is God calling you, He will make it plain." How He did this is testimony to the truth of this Scripture, "In all your ways acknowledge Him, and *He* will *Direct* your paths." (Proverbs 3:6)

At this time, the one thing I longed for most was to be full time in music ministry. I thought that was what the Lord had for me. While traveling back home after a month-long stint with Youth For Christ in Cape Town, Merle and I stopped overnight in the picturesque Town of George, to break the 12-hour car journey to East London. There I received a phone call from YFC's National Director, Dennis' house. He sounded excited! "Guess what, Noel!" he said, "our national music director has resigned, and we want you to take over his position." What I had longed for was now available—working for the Lord full time in the music ministry. But, surprise, surprise! Strange to relate, that instead of responding to Dennis with a joyful "Yes" I felt as if an invisible *hand* was holding me back from stepping onto the bus that would take me where, up to that minute, I had longed to go . . . the role of full-time musical director. To Dennis' surprise, and my own, I declined the kind offer.

A short time after this, the Lord led the local minister and elders of the East London Assembly to take me on part-time as trainee minister. In that situation my ministry in the Word grew, while I continued with the music ministry in the local church. By means of a correspondence Bible course, on-the-job training, and copious doses of God's grace, I continued to progress. After two years I was sent to Grahamstown, a small university town just over a hundred miles away from home, to take up ministry in the (very) small congregation (15 strong, including the children!) that had just recently been planted there.

Again, we see God's grace in evidence! I found myself, a real novice, ministering to highly educated young men and women, some of whom were studying theology and philosophy, who used words like eschatology, ecclesiology, pneumatology and the like, words I only vaguely understood as having something to do with our faith, and church life! Yet, several got soundly converted to Christ, and more were baptized with the Holy Spirit during our three years there. Some have been involved ministry-wise at international levels, and several are still in touch with us, serving the Lord strongly after 30-something years! Oh yes, and during the process, I also learned what eschatology, ecclesiology, pneumatology and other such-like words mean!

Looking back, it is clear to me that the Lord directed me *away* from music and into the ministry as pastor and teacher of the Word. A fair number of growing believers, is evidence of that fact.

Looking for God's guidance in your life? Don't sit around, just waiting for His call. While you pray, do what you can faithfully, whole heartedly. I gave myself fully to what I knew, the music ministry, and He directed my steps from there. Acknowledge Him as your Lord, fully in charge of your life. You will experience His Divine direction, not necessarily into full-time service, but certainly into that job that He has for you.

VERY IMPORTANT

An open door of opportunity is not always God's leading. Take my case: if I had gone with the YFC offer, I would probably never have developed a ministry in the Word. The post of music director was highly specialized, while others did the preaching and teaching. With the open door, look for the inner witness of the Spirit of God. He will nudge you forward, or He will restrain you, as He did with me.

CHAPTER 2
LEARNING GOD'S WAYS

Traveling back from a conference with my Senior Pastor, John Stelling, I hoped to impress him by reciting verses that I had memorized from Psalm 103. When I got to verse 7, "He made known His ways to Moses, His acts to the children of Israel," John, a quiet man and deeply dedicated to the Lord, posed this question to me. "Which would you rather know, God's ways or God's acts?" This question provoked me to serious thinking, just as John intended it would.

Israel, you will remember, experienced the Lord's miracle workings in their deliverance from Egypt. They had firsthand experience of God's great acts: the 10 plagues, the parting of the Red Sea for them to cross on dry land, the daily instant breakfast, Manna from heaven, and so on. However, that did not stop them from grumbling, complaining and criticizing their leaders, with disastrous consequences for them as a people.

Moses prayed, "Lord, show me Your *ways*." (Exodus 33:15) God did that. Moses stands out through the centuries as a godly, selfless leader of a troublesome people, a man to whom the Almighty spoke *face to face*! (Numbers 12:3) How would you answer John Stelling's question?

I would like to know *both* God's acts of power and His ways. But, if I only have a choice of one, I would choose His ways. For His ways lead us to more godly character and conduct. Knowing His ways leads us to greater faith, greater consecration, and a clearer and clearer likeness to Jesus Christ, our Savior.

HOW CAN WE LEARN HIS WAYS?

We must display the right attitude. Psalm 25:9 states: "The humble He guides in justice, and the humble He teaches His way."

What is humility? It is not what is displayed in this little story: A certain church held a month-long competition to see who was the most humble member of that congregation. One guy patiently tolerated all kinds of nonsense throughout the month. He wanted that badge, "Humblest Man in the Church." Finally, the day arrived, and he was awarded the badge, "Humblest Man." The next week, however, they took it away from him! Reason? *He wore it!* Yes, humility is not something to be paraded, like a badge. Nor is it something we would talk about as in: "I am really learning to be more humble. Have you noticed?"

Another story: A dear brother in Christ was always praying in the prayer meetings, "O Lord, I am the Chief of sinners," intending to echo Paul's confession of his past life before conversion. One night as the dear man yet again uttered his preamble, "I am the Chief of sinners," an elder said, "Lord, please deal with this man's pride!"

This is how I see it. Humility is not a matter of talk, or of putting ourselves down. It is simply to have a right assessment of ourselves, that before God we are nothing and we deserve nothing. Yet, He loves us and sent His Son to take the judgment we deserved for our pride and self-centeredness. It means we do not take ourselves so seriously, but we *do* take Christ seriously, as well as others.

OUR GREAT, PERFECT MODEL

Philippians 2:5 points us to Christ, the great model and example of true humility. It tells us we should have the attitude Christ displayed, in voluntarily laying aside His glory, becoming a servant, and submitting willingly to death on *The Cross*—a disgraceful form of execution in those days. Some marks of true humility!

We are more other-centered than self-centered. (Philippians 2:3-4 PARAPHRASED) States: "Consider others more important than ourselves" and "Don't look only on your own interests, but also on the interests of others." A truly humble person doesn't talk much about humility. Such a person is not gloomy, miserable, morbid, or a spoilsport. Jesus, "meek and humble in heart," was nice to be with. People invited Him to their parties. Children felt comfortable with Him. A humble person is not a weak pushover.

Jesus, humble in heart, confronted the religious leaders with their hypocrisy, called them a brood of snakes, and denounced them as blind leaders of the blind! Nothing weak about that, you agree! See Him also in the temple, trashing the money changers' tables, chasing out the animals that were sold there at exorbitant prices, and denouncing the traders as people who turned His Father's House into a den of thieves. "Gentle Jesus, meek and mild?" Humility is not weakness. When the Father's honour was attacked, Jesus went into action, we might say, "punitive action." But, when personally attacked, He did not retaliate. He was not vengeful, He did not threaten, "I'll see you on judgment day!" A humble person is always prepared to listen to correction, even if the person giving the correction is not nice about it. Remember, the Lord even used a donkey to correct the naughty prophet Balaam! The humble person tries to look past personal issues to see if the Lord is there, wanting to correct him on some issue. Such a person is one who, like Moses, can learn God's ways.

After nearly 50 years as a Christian, I am still learning. I don't always get it right, pride raises its ugly head, and with it, resentment, "they don't appreciate me" and sometimes a childish desire to impress, and so regain lost ground, as it were. But, God has a way of correcting that. James writes, "God *resists* the proud and gives *grace* to the humble." I can tell you first hand, it's not good to try to resist God, He will *always* win! If you don't humble yourself, God will humble you, and that, let me tell you, is *not nice*! Best is, run to *The Cross*, get a fresh vision of the *Perfect One* who exchanged places with you and me and suffered in our stead. That's a great antidote to pride! His way is not the worlds way. He takes weak things, pours His grace into them, and uses them to confound the strong, and the worldly wise. Our very weakness, accompanied by faith, attracts the Lord's enabling grace. My prayer is like that of Moses "Lord show me Your ways, teach me Your ways." Then, let's humbly and joyously *live* in His way, let's *walk* in His ways. For "His way is perfect" (Psalm 18:30) and "The way of the Lord is strength for the upright." (Proverbs 10:29)

CHAPTER 3
FIVE NOTABLE WOMEN

———⟨∾⟩———

Have you heard this saying: "God made women both beautiful, and foolish. He made them beautiful, that men would love them. He made them foolish, that they would love men?" Many men are indebted to some woman, or more than one, for their loving sacrificial, nurturing and inspiring role in the man's development. Sadly, we don't often give credit to the ladies for doing that.

I want to pay tribute to *Five Notable Women* who each played an important part in my life along the way. All beautiful, in looks and in spirit—and *Definitely* not foolish!

MY MOTHER—Priscilla Maria

From my earliest memories as a child, Mom was very caring, though not often physically demonstrative. I learned from her that Jesus loved me, that He died for our sins, and that we should try to please Him because we would one day stand before Him to be judged on how we behaved. Mother was a fine piano player. I used to love lying on a blanket by the piano while she played a whole range of tunes — from ragtime (Twelfth Street Rag) through romantic love songs (I Dream of Jeanie, I'll Walk Beside You) to the grand old hymns like Rock of Ages, What a Friend We Have in Jesus. I particularly remember a song she played called "Cathedral Chimes." How fascinating to me, that she made the piano sound just like church bells when she played this one! But, the one song she played and sang often, that made the biggest impression on me was the hymn, "Jesus Loves Me." These words were embedded in my mind from the earliest days, "Jesus loves me this I know, for the Bible tells me so." It had a two-fold effect: the one, that the Savior loved me personally, and two, that the Bible was a very special Book. It told the story of Jesus and His love for me. So, I was privileged to grow up in a God-fearing, Bible respecting home, although my parents didn't attend church.

NOT ALWAYS "HOME, SWEET HOME!"

However, ours wasn't always a happy home. I was a "last-lammertjie." That's Afrikaans for a child born to older parents, literally, "a late lamb." Dad, although generally a kind man, was often insensitive to Mom, making sarcastic jokes about her and her family, and laughing at her when she became angry and then dissolved into tears. As the last of the four children still in the family home, I used to hear all this, sad to report, I had very little respect for my father as a result. In spite of the hurt, Mom stayed with Dad for more than 60 (yes, 60!) years until death took her at age 79. The fact that she became truly saved while in her early 50's probably had a lot to do with that.

CHANGE HAPPENS!

Happily, I can report that, in their last few years together Dad mellowed toward her. I think a major turning point came when they became victims of a vicious home invasion incident. Dad had to sit helplessly looking on while one of the low-life thugs beat Mom repeatedly, hoping to get Dad to divulge where the money was kept. (Vain hope, they never had much money!) We wondered if Mom would survive the attack. Over a period of a few months she recovered, and resumed her characteristic role serving her husband as wife and help meet. Through it all she continued to trust the Lord and praise Him for all His goodness.

Mom's influence on me?

- A deep respect, appreciation (and sympathy) for women, especially mothers.
- A love for Christ and His Word.
- A gift of musical ability. I played the piano, and for several years, earned a living teaching music.

A ROMAN CATHOLIC NUN–Sister Hubble

Her involvement in my life was brief, but came at a crucial time. My parents told me that, at birth, there was a good chance that I would not make it. I don't know what the problem was. I think you will understand, I was too young to know! Desperate to save the life of their fourth child, my parents took me to the Mater Dei, a Catholic hospital in our home town East London. There, Sister Hubble agreed to take me in as her personal responsibility. "On one condition," she told Mom and Dad "that you do not call me. I will call you when I think it fit to do so." As I recall the story, I was exclusively her patient for several months, she literally became my "mother." Before she called my parents and told them to come and fetch their child, now completely well. The report I had was that she handed me back to my parents with this charge: "God has spared your son and made him well. Be sure you give him back to God." Maybe this was prophetic. At any rate, as early as I can remember, I was conscious of the Lord, and, though salvation only became actual to me when I passed the age of 20, I always had a strong desire to serve Him in some way. You may be asking: "What about your 'temporary mother?' " Regrettably, I never got to talk to this blessed lady. By the time I was old enough to have done so, Sister Hubble had moved to a Catholic home for retired nuns in Johannesburg, about 600 miles from East

London. Mom made sure I sent her a greeting card every year at Christmas time. The dear lady passed away while I was yet quite young. Her Influence? God used her to save my life! She did this for a family she had never met, and that she never again saw after I was made well. Sacrificial service, for Jesus sake.

MUSIC TEACHER–Cooksie Kaserzon

Cooksie Kaserzon was a very attractive and musically talented young Jewish woman. She won national awards as a piano accordionist, she was an accomplished pianist and electronic organist, and she had a music school which I joined in my late teens, to learn piano. Up until then, I played mainly by ear, trying to imitate Mom's style, for my own amusement. (Some wag suggested that, playing by ear could become quite painful, I should rather use my hands!) Within a short time Cooksie had me playing for charity shows and dances, and then she pulled me in to play with her at local hotels at Sundowner time. (Cocktail Hour if you prefer!) If I say so myself, we played *nice* music! We were popular! Cooksie played Hammond organ, I played piano, and we had a drummer to provide the rhythm for our mix of George Gershwin, Cole Porter and such-like ballads, with the occasional Rhumba or Samba thrown in. I loved it! I must add, I also like being paid for playing! Cooksie then brought me into the school to teach piano. When she left East London to marry and live in Johannesburg, she *gave* me the piano section of her school. I paid *nothing* for the business, not even for the piano that she left me with! Though not big, the studio kept me eating for a few years, even into marriage, until I became a trainee pastor, whereupon I sent off some of my pupils to another music teacher in town.

COOKSIE'S INFLUENCE?

By helping me develop as a musician, she showed by her actions the value of investing unselfishly in younger people. My contribution to her, and to her career, was *minimal*! I was virtually the sole beneficiary of our relationship! Yet, she continuously gave herself unstintingly to my musical development, without complaint. She was like a big sister to me, and I regret that we did not keep in contact when she moved away. As I write about her, I am stirred afresh to give the Lord thanks for putting this Jewess—one of His chosen people, in my life at a critical juncture.

SPIRITUAL MOTHER–Mary Mullan

Mary Mullan was, to put it mildly, a colourful character. Part Jewish (on her mother's side) when still a young woman she got converted at a Gospel meeting somewhere in England. When she told her

Mom—"I'm saved!" Her mother is reported to have said "you've never been lost," took away her privileges as daughter, and put her to work as the family maid in the family's middle class British residence, without pay, I believe! Nothing daunted, Mary maintained her Christian testimony, and not long after this, married James Mullan, a fiery Irishman who had come from atheism to salvation. Soon after their wedding, this pair of radicals sailed for Africa where they served as missionaries in the Congo jungle for a number of years. While there Mary gave birth to Sheila, the first of their five daughters. The couple faced many hardships and dangers in the Congo. Their first "home" was a tiny house of mud and wattle walls, thatched roof and mud floors. Security, if one could call it that—was almost nonexistent. They had to rely totally on a faithful God for protection. Once, baby Sheila was snatched away just in time from a snake that had slithered right up to her where she was playing outside near her mother. Another time, when Jim was away on ministry, Mary woke up in the middle of the night to see by candlelight a snake crawling up the sleeping babies cot. Hell hath no fury, like a woman whose baby is threatened! Mary beat the serpent to death with a stick she found nearby.

The most remarkable account of their troubles, and of the Lord's intervention was when Mary was struck by lightning during a thunderstorm. The thatched roof of their little house was on fire, and

Mary was flat on the ground, "lights out!" In response to her husband's desperate prayer, she recovered sufficiently to hold the baby while he pulled them both out of danger. However, she was unable to speak until Jim had prayed once more. Miraculously, his wife was healed, and carried on having babies and serving the Lord! We didn't neglect to use this story against Mary at strategic times, when we didn't quite agree with her on a given subject. "Sister Mullan," we would say "you were struck by lightning, remember perhaps that is why you can't think straight on this issue!" I need to point out: in those days our Pentecostal Christian culture required us to call each other "brother" or "sister" as a mark of respect and affection. That's how come I called my spiritual mother "Sister Mullan!"

MEETING WITH MARY

My association with this remarkable woman began soon after my conversion. Jim and Mary had by then left the Congo, and were being used of God to plant churches in South Africa. They were based at this time in my home town East London and Mary became part of my choir. Because of who she was (and who she was married to) I consulted her regularly about the music I had to arrange for the meetings. These sessions regularly "morphed" into discipleship moments, as she pointed me to relevant Scriptures and gave counsel on serious matters that concerned me as a young believer. When Merle and I married, Mary was there for Merle when she needed advice as a young bride. I must point out, my bride and I had precisely *no* formal premarital counsel. We read books, and after our wedding Merle talked to Mary, and then shared with me afterwards what had been said! But, please, don't feel sorry for us *we enjoyed* learning and finding things out for ourselves!

NOT A DIPLOMAT!

In paying tribute to this woman, my spiritual Mom, I have to say, Mary was no diplomat. "Subtle" was not her style, nor was it ever a word in her vocabulary! Like an old-fashioned mother, she told you straight out "That's Wrong!" "No, you can't do that! If you want to serve God, you have to stop doing this." "You wouldn't ask that question if you had been reading your Bible" and so on. No molly-coddling! I appreciated that. One always knew for sure where you stood, or—where you *should* be standing! Now, don't get the idea that Mary had a face and a personality baptized in vinegar. On the contrary, she had a truly vivacious smile, she had a keen sense of humour and a delightfully contagious laugh, she was truly fun to be with. These qualities she retained even to her old age. Here's a sample. After losing touch with her for some years, I finally ended up ministering in the town where she was living in an old age residence. She was in her late 70's by this time. I made an appointment to call on her, and she came back with this remark: "Bring your wife with you, we don't want the neighbours to talk!"

MARY'S INFLUENCE

Mary Mullan imbued me with a passion for pleasing God, no matter what it cost. She and Jim were outstanding examples of consistent selfless sacrificial service, of unswerving devotion to Jesus and to His church. Consider: how else could they have done what they did? They left England right after they were married, and settled, (SETTLED?) in the jungles of the Belgian Congo. Then, in their later years, they gave themselves to pioneer the work of God in South Africa, staying only a few years in a town until the new church they had planted was established in the faith, before moving on to new fields. I was always impressed by their example. Then, Mary taught me, and demonstrated by her life, the paramount importance of the Bible as the sole guide to Christian living. Opinions on issues were always tested by her question: "What does the Bible say about this?" Lastly, her life taught me "Take God *very* seriously, but don't take yourself too seriously!" She laughed a lot, often at herself— a powerful example of this axiom. I hope I've been a worthy "son," dear mother Mary!

MY WIFE–Merle

I've saved the best for last! The fifth notable woman in my life is of course, my wife Merle. This year end Merle and I will celebrate our 50th wedding anniversary, God willing. Through all those years she has manifested the qualities we read about in Proverbs 31, describing the virtuous woman. I am so blessed to have her as my life's partner, and mother of our three children, Delray, Stephen and Mark. Born Merle Florence Devonshire in Walvis Bay, South West Africa (now Namibia) in 1941, Merle had a less—than—perfect upbringing. Her father Tom was a deep-sea diver, and was actually decorated by King George of England for his services with the allies during World War II. Tom married three times. His first wife, Merle's mom Betty, married twice, and Merle attended 16 different schools during her childhood years. She was often "tossed" between her parents during the school vacations. In fact, on one occasion they just didn't show up to take her home for the holidays. After a fruitless wait in the hallway, the little girl just had to stay with the nuns at the boarding school for the duration of the holidays.

I ask you, how would you rate the chances of this child growing up undamaged psychologically and emotionally? Yet, through nearly 50 years, this lady has been a spiritual nurturer of hundreds, both men and women, through her example and her Bible based counseling ministry. All of this of course in addition to being a top class mother and now greatly loved grandma to Bianca and Joel. Hail—Super-Mom!

Of course, it didn't start out like that! The Lord takes time to form His workers. Merle was converted to Christ in her early teens, while boarding with my brother Joe, his wife Stella, and their two daughters, Rita and Valerie. Joe's radical conversion and deliverance from alcohol set the ball rolling in our family, and Merle was part of that batch of converts. I took a few years to catch up, *you see*, I was a clean-living, God-fearing guy, bound up at that stage with my self-righteousness. I couldn't therefore acknowledge the need to *surrender* my life to Jesus "tho" I believed in Him and knew that He loved me. After all, I wasn't a drunken sinner like my brother had been! I really fancied this pretty 14-year-old chick who was technically my step-cousin. (Her Dad's third wife was my Aunt Issie, Mom's sister.) But, Merle left school and moved back to Namibia to work there. We kept in touch by letter, but only came together a few years later when she moved to Cape Town and I traveled the 600 miles alone by car to find her! From then on the pace quickened, and we were married in East London about a year later.

NOT A DIARY, BUT A TRIBUTE!

This was just background. I do not intend to set out a year-by-year account of our life together. Rather, I want to give honour to my wife, highlighting some of the many qualities she has displayed through the years, qualities that make her an accurate modern-day edition of the Proverbs 31 woman. In the course of our 44 years in the ministry, pastoring 12 different congregations, we have had to move house, hold your breath—15 (that's right 15) times! Through all of this Merle has never complained. She has always rapidly transformed the new place of residence into a pleasant, comfortable home, and then worked on the yard to turn an often barren piece of ground into a colourful showpiece. (I *did* help, from time-to-time!) Merle has always been very industrious. She's always looking for ways to generate income. She is the money person in the marriage.

OPEN HOME

A constant feature of our ministry has been the ministry of hospitality. From the very beginning we were having people around, sometimes for tea, more often for meals. These were never intended to be mere social occasions. Then, as now, we always used them as ministry opportunities—for informal testimonies, for low-key teachings from the Word. After all, if you come to my home and eat my food, you must also let me put some spiritual food down your mouth, right! For all this Merle does the catering and cooking, with some help from some of the guests from time-to-time.

PROVERBS 31 INDEED!

Here is a selection of verses from this chapter that epitomize my wife in her role as wife, mother, and minister of God.

- vs 10 Who can find a virtuous wife? I have found her! Indeed, she is worth far more than rubies, diamonds, gold or silver!
- vs 11 The heart of her husband safely trusts her. She is completely loyal as my wife, and as partner in the greatest enterprise on earth—the Christian ministry.
- vs 12 She does him good and not evil all the days of her life. This is the benefit I have derived from having this woman in my life.
- vs 13 She seeks wool and flax and willingly works with her hands and is very industrious. Merle is very skilled in craftwork.
- vs 15 She rises while it is yet night and provides food for her household.
- vs 16 She considers a field and buys it. From her profits she plants a vineyard. She is a good business woman.
- vs 26 She opens her mouth with wisdom and on her tongue is the law of kindness. She is not a chatterbox, she doesn't "nag," and she is never unkind. Therefore, many people—men as well as women—seek her out for counsel.
- vs 27 She watches over the ways of her

household and does not eat the bread of idleness. She is an excellent homemaker and mother.

Therefore:

• vs 28 Her children rise up and call her blessed.

Our children rightly regard her as the Queen. They think she qualifies easily for the title "Super-Mum!"

CHAPTER 4
MARRIAGE, AS WE KNOW IT

I often say, the two greatest gifts God has given me are:
- My Saviour, the Lord Jesus Christ.
- My wife, my marriage partner.

Today we are seeing the devaluing and deconstruction of marriage and family. This is of great concern to me, because the Bible says: "Let marriage be held in highest honour." (Hebrews 13:4) Let me share with you marriage as we know it from our 50 years of experience, and from the teachings of the Bible. Firstly, marriage originates with the Creator, it is not some invention of Man. Genesis chapter 1 records the creation of humankind, "He created them male and female." (Genesis 1:27) In Genesis 2 we have a kind of action replay of the account with a little more detail. Here we read that He first created Adam, gave him a job cultivating and guarding the garden, and representing his Maker in taking dominion over the animal world.

SOMETHING'S MISSING HERE!

After watching him for a while the Lord God said in effect: This guy needs help, he's not shaping up too well. So, the Lord created the woman from some part taken out of Adam while he was sleeping under Divine anesthetic. When he woke up and saw this stunningly beautiful two-legged creature standing before him, he exclaimed: "Woo—Man!" That's how the female human got to be known as "woman!" Well, that's my rather loose modern translation of all that went on as recorded in Genesis 2:18-23. Notice, this is recorded as the first *marriage*. Verse 25 refers to "the man and his WIFE. . ." It's of great importance to note that Jesus publicly endorsed this passage in Genesis when the Pharisees asked him about divorce. "Haven't you read. . ." he said and quoted Genesis 1:27, and chapter 2:24. "He made them male and female," and "For this cause a man shall leave his father and mother [up to this point, the closest of all human relationships] and be joined to his wife, and the two shall become one flesh. . ."

THE KEY

Then, our Lord added this truth-statement which every about-to-be-married couple needs to note. It's the key to marital harmony. "So then they are *no longer two* but *one flesh*." (Matthew 19:6) In our premarital sessions Merle and I always bring this point home to the couple. "Do you realize" we say, "that when you take your vows, you are giving away your independence?" "They are *no longer two*," said Jesus. At this point in the session, the groom might go pale as he suddenly faces this fact: he is not just adding this luscious creature to his lifestyle to improve it, he is abandoning his independence. He is replacing the word "Me" with the word "We" in all his considerations. Of course, the same goes for the bride-to-be. This point needs to be emphasized strongly because so much marital conflict ensues when one, or both of the parties still have the "I want it *my* way" mentality. Realizing that we are no longer two we will always be wanting to work for the good of the marriage, even thou it may only come at the cost of personal inconvenience. Of course, this has got to be two-way traffic. Sometimes you have to give in, at other times your spouse has to yield. What matters is that *both* of you recognize that you're a team, and that everything you do should work for the good of the team. To put it bluntly. The marriage comes first. "They are no longer two, but one. . ."

NOT A MINDLESS AUTOMATON

Now, in case this unasked question is buzzing around in your mind—let me state it for you, and then give the *happy* answer.

Question: does this mean that I lose my individuality and just become like some automaton, with no right to express my personality? Answer: NOT-AT-ALL! You bring who you are into the marriage. Your will must be bent towards the "We" of your partnership. Your unique personality, surrendered to Christ, is needed to make an essential contribution to the "team." Merle has a very good business head, with a mind for details. I am slack when it comes to that and I find details really irksome. Imagine the mess we would have if she buried this aspect of who she is, "for the sake of peace." We would be in a total mess if she didn't make her contribution to the team in this regard. Conversely, think of what the marriage would be like if it was all business like and precise, with many tiresome details. See, both parties need to bring their gifts to the partnership, to complement each other. Some have remarked that, for our marriage to have endured so well for so long, we must be perfectly compatible. Not so! In fact, with our contrasting personalities, we can be more accurately described as comBatible! (Don't know if that's a word in the dictionary. But, it fits what I'm trying to explain!) But in every instance (although we sometimes have to retreat for a brief cooling-off period) we always aim for what's best for the team.

JUST A WORD ABOUT FIGHTING NICELY!

In the best of marriages, conflicts will occur. How we handle these conflicts is of critical importance. In any marital verbal scuffle, *do not* attack the person, address the *issue*. Don't say: "There you go again! You are so inconsiderate—you never think of my feelings in any situation!" This will very likely bring a not-so-nice reaction, perhaps like this: "And what about you? You always. . ." and so the conflict escalates. Rather, say something like this: "I have a problem, and I need your help. When you say [or do] so-and-so—I feel demeaned. Please don't do that." This approach, while direct, is softer and more likely to open the way to talk through a problem instead of waging war and wounding each other with harsh words.

TWO NO-NO WORDS

Notice, in the above illustration I used two words we must *never* use in a verbal skirmish, they will *always* make matters worse. These two words are *always* and *never*. They usually cause a negative, defensive comeback. Example: You may say, "you always forget to do such-and-such" your partner will likely retaliate in this way: "and what about you? I suppose you never. . ." and so the argument escalates, and the devil laughs! Remember, you as a couple are on the same team you want to do what's best for the team. On the playing field team members don't kick each other, they go for the opposing team! If problems arise, the coach tries to sort out the problem off the field, for the well being of the team! Am I being repetitive? You're right, I am! If marriage partners will "fight nicely" we won't have so many unhappy marriages. So, let me say again, when arguments arise, *do not* attack the person, explain the issue. If things are getting hot—back off, have a time-out, but come back again to talk *with*, not *at* each other. Remember the Beatitude "Blessed are the peacemakers," be one, a *peacemaker*, not a *peacebreaker*!

AT LEAST ONE SMART MOVE!

As a young husband, I regret to admit I didn't do many things right. We were both learning this "marriage" thing, while at the same time I was striving to establish myself in the ministry. As I look back on those early years, I thank the Lord for His patience with me, and for Merle's unswerving devotion even when I was so insensitive to her needs at times. There was one thing that I did right early on. I said to my wife, there are two words that do not exist in our vocabulary *separation* and *divorce*. We married because we loved each other, and our vows, taken before God bound us together—we were "no longer two." This was said during our ordinary conversation. Merle commented later on how much this had helped her. She explained, whenever we would have a verbal skirmish, the thought would invade her mind, "Your father and mother divorced, your brother got divorced, you're going to go the same way." When I made that statement, it closed the door in her mind through which the devil was trying to gain access. I am happy to report, we have never come even close to a crisis point in our relationship where there was a danger of breaking up. We always need to be on guard. Satan hates Christ, he hates God, and he hates marriage because it originates with God, *plus* your marriage is to be a *visible* reflection of the *mystical* union between Christ and His Bride, the True church. Hence, it is his target. As the thief Jesus referred to in John 10:10, he comes to steal to kill and to destroy. Let's not give him an opening to do this to our marriage relationship.

SO WHO'S THE BOSS?

In marriage, a Boss? No way! A boss is a person who makes decisions, gives orders and has the right to reprimand or even fire you if you don't perform acceptably. Marriage is a covenant between two equals, neither of which has the right to order the other around. There is no "boss" in a marriage. However, as on any team, there must be a leader, on every ship there must be a captain. The Bible states clearly, the husband is the Head of the wife. We must notice two truths here.
- Headship is *not* dominance.
- Submission does not denote inferiority.

The husband is the Head of the wife as *Christ* is the Head of the Body, the church. This means the husband is to show his love for his wife to the point of sacrificing his personal preferences if this will benefit her. Christ gave Himself for the church. The wife is to submit to her husband's leadership, but not as a passive partner. She is his "help meet," his companion. Her submissive attitude does not make her an inferior partner. Notice, Jesus was submissive to God the Father. He stated, "I do always the things that please Him." He was in no way inferior to the Father. In John 5:23, He said "That all men should honour the Son even as they honour the Father." The wife has equal status, equal honour with her husband. Both were created in the image and likeness of God, remember! But, the husband has the responsibility to lead, to make decisions for the welfare of the marriage. With him rests the final responsibility before God.

HOW THIS WORKS WITH US

On most issues Merle and I consult with each other. Sometimes we don't agree, but unless she has a strong conscientious objection, we agree to do it my way. On other occasions having listened to her side of the matter, I make the decision "We'll do it your way." After all she *is* a smart lady! So, what if it doesn't work out well? I don't say "See, I shouldn't have listened to you. Now look at the mess you've got us into!" As the Head of the family, I took the decision to do it her way. I cannot blame her, I say rather "we got it wrong." Sometimes when we fail to agree, Merle brings into play her axiom "If you can't back the *plan*, back the *man*." One incident stands out which gives my wife credit, and shows me up in less than a good light. (Some of you will really like that!)

Our son Stephen, home on pass from the Army for the weekend, asked to borrow the car. Merle said "No" quite forcefully. I felt he needed a break to go out with some friends, so I said "yes." Well, he took the car (I'm the Head, remember?) and drove off with a cheerful "thanks Dad." A few hours later I received a phone call. Steve had collided with a very solid object, he was in the hospital and our car was a write off! We got our son back, but had to get a new car!

NOT A "HARPIST"

To this day, Merle has *never* reproached me with "I told you so—you should have listened to me!" For this I am truly grateful. Another woman might have harped on this for years, to the detriment of the relationship. However, through that experience I have learned to be a bit more alert when my wife raises a strong objection to any decision I am making. Very often after I have looked at the issue more closely, I decide, "You're right dear, let's do it your way." So often she's been right and I have been proved smart to go with her decision! But, I take the responsibility for doing so. This is how we see the Headship of the husband. This is how it works for us.

SOME PRACTICAL MARRIAGE FRESHENERS

At all times we treat each other with respect. We never hold the other person up to ridicule. I never allowed our children to disrespect their mother. The penalty for doing so was always severe—very severe! We always say "please" and "thank you" for any favour, whether big or small. "Thanks for ironing my shirts, thanks for taking out the garbage, for clearing up the dishes . . . I appreciate the trouble you've taken to help me with. . ." Whether I've been out of the house for the day, or for just a few hours, we always greet each other warmly with a peck on the cheek. This applies when either of us leaves the house too. When we go walking anywhere, we usually hold hands. This is not so that people can say, "Oh look, isn't that sweet!" Yes, it *is* sweet! But, we hold hands because we *like* each other, we like to be together, and that's one of the many ways to show it. We are generous with compliments, on dress, on performance, on kind acts. Caution, we are sincere and honest, we never flatter each other. In the main, we dress to please each other. "Do you like this dress [blouse, jersey] on me?" she asks. If I answer "no" she takes it off and tries another. For my part, I too like to wear what she likes me to wear. She has good taste! Men, take note! Here's a warning for you! One time she said "How do you like this dress on me?" Looks fine, I said, preoccupied with something else. "When I showed you this one last month you said you didn't like it!" was her come back! Lesson: In matters like this, *pay attention*! *Remember* what you endorsed verbally, or rejected, and be *consistent*!

CHAPTER 5
NOTABLE MEN WHO HAVE HELPED SHAPE MY LIFE

The writer of Proverbs states: "He who walks with wise men will be wise." This underlines the importance of keeping good company, of having close relationships with people whose influence can do you good. I have had the good fortune to have certain men in my life who have exerted a positive influence on me, at different stages of my earthly pilgrimage.

MY BROTHER–Jack

As mentioned before, I was a "laat lammertjie" born 20 years after my eldest brother Joe. My dad was more like a kindly grandfather to me and Jack, the second eldest son, played the father role. As I remember, from about the age of 10 he began spending time with me by taking me to sporting events. I particularly recall regularly watching him playing tennis with friends and in summer I attended the cricket matches he played in so that my love for ball games was nurtured.

At age 13, Jack had me playing in the men's 3rd League Team with him—a big step up for a shy, skinny, little boy. But, what I lacked in physical size, I made up for with passion and a certain amount of skill, and in time I began to turn in a few good performances with both bat and ball. Within a few years, under my brother's tutelage I had graduated to the 2nd League. By age 18, I was selected to join a squad of young men (all under 23 years of age), to be specially coached with the prospect of later on playing at provincial level. It was around this time that my music career began to conflict with my sport, so, sports had to go. One reason was, as a pianist, I couldn't risk hurting my hands catching a hard cricket ball bare-handed. You baseball fans must know, we cricketers don't use even one glove in the field of play, we do it all with bare hands. (Applause please! Please? Okay, then, Let's move on!) Only the batters and the wicket-keeper (the catcher behind the batter) use gloves and other protection.

Jack, you must know, had serious health issues as a boy. While in his teens, he suffered a botched throat operation that damaged his vocal chords. From then on, he was only ever able to speak with a soft, rasping voice, something akin to a person just coming out of a severe bout of laryngitis. In addition to that, as a youngster he caught double pneumonia twice and lived his last 40-something years with only one lung functioning!

Yet, this heroic brother of mine ran his own fresh produce business, lifted weights, played tennis and cricket, and lived a very productive, active life until in his early 50's. By then, the strain on his only lung began to tell and he steadily grew weaker and less active.

NOT ONLY THE SPORTING FIELD

Jack's influence over me did not only extend to the area of sport. He modeled for me what gentlemanly behavior was, both on and off the field of play. He didn't say much, he didn't have to. I learned by seeing how he behaved on the field when things didn't go well, never losing his temper, never querying an umpire's decision.

I learned how to behave in female company by showing respect and doing courteous acts like, opening the car door for a lady and getting up from your seat to greet one if she walked into the room. He taught me respect for women, and he showed me by his quiet example how to behave among older people. Though not a confessing Christian at that stage, he modeled the Golden Rule: "Do unto others as you would have them do unto you." (Matthew 7:12)

Most importantly, I learned from Jack, and his wife Molly, the beauty of a good marriage. Because of what I saw in them, even before I reached my teens, I was dreaming of the day when I would marry and settle down to the blessing of sharing life with "my special person!"

THE BIRDS AND THE BEES?

The one thing we never touched on was the subject of sex. The closest we got to talking about the birds and the bees was when still a preteenager, just before the birth of their first child Alan. I asked Jack, "Why is the Doctor visiting Molly these last few days?" He answered, "She's having a baby, but it's not the sort of thing chaps talk about." That settled the matter for me "guys don't talk about it!" Of course, I was later to discover that among my small exclusive circle of friends, guys *did* talk about it . . . quite a lot!

To sum up, my brother Jack never formally sat down with me to instruct me on any matter. He taught me "on the move," as it were, as situations arose. He modeled true manliness and courage in the way he functioned efficiently and uncomplainingly, in business and on the sporting field, and in spite of his condition, which I have already described.

Supremely, he modeled for me a good husband and a good father to his sons Alan, Peter and Paul. Until he died, at age 60, he and Molly were sweethearts. They often held hands in public, and sometimes even kissed in front of me—to this young boys great embarrassment! His faith in Christ was genuine, though never bold and public. I believe I'll meet him again in heaven. No one could live such a Christlike life in such testing circumstances without having the Lord to help him do so.

CHAIRMAN–John Bond

John was the longtime Chairman of the multiracial South African Assemblies of God. It is highly significant that this conservative, Christian white man, a descendant of British stock, was repeatedly voted in as Chairman of this multiracial movement, by a black majority conference, for nigh on 28 years, and this, during the apartheid era! Thus, telling of a convincing testimony to his consistent, unsullied reputation as a leader of uncompromising integrity, impartiality and godly wisdom.

My personal involvement with John began after Merle and I left the Grahamstown Assembly in 1973 and joined his Apostolic team of ministers in Cape Town. I must explain, several congregations in the Assembly of God worked independently, under the oversight of the 20-man General Executive. But, others chose to work more closely together with a particular leader under his specific oversight. They followed the pattern of Paul the apostle who worked directly with Silas, Timothy, Titus and others, and retained a fatherly care over churches he had established, like the congregations in Corinth, in Philippi, Colosse and so on. John Bond led one such group.

As time went on, his group expanded to several dozen churches and ministers (testimony to the effectiveness of his Apostolic leadership at that time). We were under John's personal oversight for more than 20 years before he stepped down voluntarily from his leadership roles both as Chairman and as leader of his group of churches. By this time, he was about 70 years old and it was a planned move in order to make way for a younger leader to emerge.

IMPACT

What impacted me from the start was his strength of character. John Bond was not flamboyant, either in dress or in manner. One got the impression of a quiet, solid rock-like figure that would not compromise on any principle of conscience in order to please people and to make peace.

Many times, I witnessed this in leadership meetings and at general conference. There were occasions when he would have won friends if he were to backpedal on an issue, but noway! With John it was never a case of "is this popular?" but, "is it *right?*" He modeled for me portions of Psalm 15.

"Who shall ascend to the hill of the Lord?
He that has clean hands and a pure heart. . .
He . . . keeps his promise even when it hurts."
(NLT ADAPTED)

Was John perfect? Of course not! There were times when we, his "under-leaders," had to point out an error. He was usually very open to such constructive criticism from his inner circle because he was sure of our loyalty. In this way, he modeled for me true humility. I learned that to admit you were wrong and to apologize did not denote weakness. Rather, it showed a selfless attitude and true strength of character. John was secure in Christ, and in his role as leader, he could take criticism even when it was unkind.

THE MAIN THING

John's preaching was, of course, always solid, straight from the Scriptures. What impacted me most forcibly was being at prayer with him. Whether he was leading in prayer at a conference of hundreds, at a Sunday church service, or praying with just a few of us leaders in our home, it nearly always had this effect on me, I felt I was with a man who was much further into the Holy of Holies in God's Presence than I could ever be!

He prayed with a passion that was stirring. Sometimes he would weep as he petitioned the Lord regarding certain needs in the Work. As I write, I remember his prayer for me one morning at a ministers' meeting: "Lord, help him to *grow*, help him to *grow*!" (His emphasis, not mine!) I realized then that my immaturity must have been showing quite prominently! I think the Lord is still busy answering John's prayer! (I suspect Merle is also still presenting this petition to the Lord for me!)

The impact of those times of prayer with him has been significant and lasting. As a result, my prayers are not often polite requests—that's okay, of course. Rather, I am stirred to *call* on God, to pray *fervently*, passionately, using the Scriptures a lot as the basis of my prayers.

MEMORABLE SNIPPETS

John Bond had an impish sense of humor that often came out at unexpected times. At one conference there was serious discussion about the merits of the King James Bible with its 17th Century English, over against the more modern translations. Some felt strongly that the King James was the *only* Bible for us—that we should not tamper with that old and venerated translation. John, presenting the argument that language changes rendered some words in the King James unintelligible, referred to a verse in Jeremiah that mentions a vision the prophet had of a basket of "naughty figs." His face crinkled up as he reflected mischievously, "I wonder what those figs were up to?" That nearly brought the house down and eased some of the tension that had been developing! Of course, the point was a modern version translates "naughty figs" as figs gone bad or overripe!

Back in the 60's, and even the 70's, the Pentecostal churches frowned on the practice of Christian women wearing make-up. It was considered to be "of the world," which we are not allowed to love, nor copy.

John caused a stir by saying from the pulpit: "There's nothing wrong with a bit of make-up. Even an old barn needs a bit of paint from time-to-time!" He was denounced by some of his older colleagues for this and other similar statements. They accused him of going "liberal" a *bad* word in Pentecostal circles. Many of the women in our congregations loved him for it. Although, they weren't too thrilled about the "old barn" analogy!

On the vexing question of why some people are healed and others are not (and the fact that this could discourage us from praying for the sick) I heard him say, "If I pray for 99 people and none of them are healed, when number 100 comes for prayer, I will pray in faith. Why? Because, the Bible tells me to pray for the sick." That, for him, settled any questions of doubt, just do what the Bible says and trust God to do what He wants to do.

YOUR ARE THE ONLY ONE WHO CAN HELP IN THIS SITUATION!

This was John's plea to me when he wanted us to move, often at very short notice, to a new Assembly. The way things worked in those days: If we had been in a certain location for say, 3 to 5 years, and another church somewhere in the country was in need, then, we were asked to move there. In one way it was almost flattering—John looked to us to help steady up a congregation that was weak and ailing or had suffered a spiritually crippling blow. He called us in to bring healing and growth again. It worked some of the time, at least!

On the other hand it was hard for us as a family,

especially when our three children had to change schools so often. During our 30-something years in the ministry in South Africa, we moved house 14 times! The girls, Merle and daughter Delray, always adjusted to the move quite quickly. Me and the boys, Stephen and Mark—not so quickly!

However, the Lord always brought us through and we, honestly, have no regrets. It was a privilege to serve the Lord under John Bond's leadership. Through the years, when we want to press someone into doing something inconvenient, the family often says with a smile: "You're the *only* one who can help in this situation!" It brings back happy memories!

CHAPTER 6
MY STATEGY FOR CHURCH GROWTH(?)!

—————⋐⋙⋑⋛⋐————

I suppose it's to be expected that I will be asked, through the years of (reasonably) fruitful ministry, "What has been your strategy for growing churches?" My answer: None! At least, not intentionally! I never sat down to formally work out a plan, nor did I have anyone taking me on a special course on the development of my own ministry as a leader. Everything I learned was "on the job," working with leaders like John Bond, and from time-to-time, other leaders whom John would bring in to teach us.

He also encouraged us to read widely and extensively. In contrast to the mind set of many in those early days, we were encouraged to read the writings of authors both inside and outside of our Pentecostal denomination. This brought us great spiritual and intellectual benefits. We learned to eat the meat and spit out the bones. I can assure you, there was a lot of meat!

So, my strategy then was as it is now: Preach the

Word, pray fervently, and love the people. Above all plans, strategies or programs, God's People need to be fed on the Scriptures. I have grown by hearing, reading and learning the Word. This is always the major factor in both personal and church growth. In 2 Timothy 4:1-2, Paul addresses Timothy in very serious, somber tones: "I charge you, therefore, before God and the Lord Jesus Christ preach the Word." The NLT translates verse 2 like this: "Preach the Word of God. Be persistent, whether the time is favourable or not. Patiently correct, rebuke and encourage your people with good teaching."

I have found in almost every case where I have stuck to the idea of the primacy of preaching God's Word, people have grown spiritually. Where a congregation was ailing, the Word brought healing and health. Where people had suffered disillusionment, the Scriptures brought about restoration of faith and of joy. Fortunately, I didn't have to be a great expounder of the Scriptures to see those results. I just prayed, showed a genuine love for the people, and told them what the Bible said. When disputes would arise, we just went back to the question: what does the Bible say about this? Then, "Let's do it!"

In our first Assembly in Grahamstown, I found myself preaching to really smart young university students, and sometimes to their lecturers. (Remember, I never finished High School!) I voiced my misgivings to Noel Scheepers, my overseer at the time. He said something like this: "Don't let that intimidate you.

You're not competing with them intellectually, you're feeding them spiritually on the Word. In that way, you are farther ahead of them." So, the little church grew. We're still in touch with some of those students from that era. Many are going on well with the Lord after nearly 40 years, and at least two have risen to prominence in international ministry.

Another illustration of the power of the preached Word. On leaving Grahamstown, we arrived in Cape Town, in the midst of a season of growth. John Bond and the Harfield Road church elders had taken the bold step of hiving off from the 350-strong congregation to plant two other churches. So, in one day, one Assembly became three Assemblies! The "mother" church had to now face up to the reality of being just about a 100 strong on Sundays, and about 50 to 60 strong at the Wednesday night Bible study. This was not easy, the previously full hall was now less than a third full. A bit depressing for those left behind, yes!

My strategy? I knew of none, so I preached the Word, prayed, and loved the people. Within about two years, we were full on Sundays. In fact, it became overcrowded. On Sunday nights I sometimes preached with half-a-dozen or more children quietly sitting or lying on the platform at my feet! They were there to leave room in the pews for the adults. Wednesday nights our Bible study grew from about 60 to over 200, sometimes reaching 250.

What was my secret? What was the attraction?

We preached and "teached" the Word, prayed and loved the people, and God gave the growth. John Bond had, of course, previously laid a good foundation there over the years, and the three Assemblies prospered. Within 10 years they had became 10 churches. In other congregations we had a more moderate success. But, one more example will serve to show the value of the regular, consistent preaching and teaching of the Scriptures.

The Somerset West Assembly was more or less crippled when we moved there. A few sweet saints were valiantly holding the fort, having experienced several severe blows in the form of demonic attacks and human (moral) failure. In just over a year, attendance and finances had turned around and increased threefold. We taught the Word, prayed and loved . . . Same old story, yes! God caused the growth.

In the United States where we now live, we have tried to maintain that three-pronged "attack," and the same on our regular ministry trips to South Africa, Malawi, England and India. I never go with any sort of novelty feature to attract the people. I go with the Scriptures, and God gives the increase!

THE SECOND PRONG IN MY "STRATEGY"
PRAY FERVENTLY AND CONSISTENTLY.

Here's a story I really like. A certain little boy, feeling rather lonely, asked his parents for a little brother. His dad, knowing something his son didn't know, wanted to use the opportunity to teach his boy the power of prayer. He suggested "Why don't you pray and ask the Lord to send you a little brother?" The boy agreed, and began his prayer journey. After a while however, he told his Father, "Dad, I've quit praying, nothing is happening." Dad encouraged him to persevere, but to no avail. Eventually, it happened! Mom came home from the hospital with not one, but two little baby brothers for the boy! His dad said "There my boy, aren't you glad you prayed?" His son looked at the two squalling infants and replied, "Dad, aren't you glad I *stopped* praying when I did?"

While a believer yet young in the faith, I somehow had the idea (subconsciously) that one had to really "psyche" oneself up to get a hearing from the Lord. A change came to me when I read two particular verses.

- (Jeremiah 31:3) Where the Lord says "I have loved you with an everlasting love. Therefore, with loving kindness I have *drawn* you." I began to realize that every impulse I had to pray basically came from the Father who was drawing me into His loving Presence.

True, our needs often drive us to pray, but the very fact that we want to take those needs to Him is testimony to this fact that His love is an invisible cable pulling us to Himself, to present our needs to Him.

- (Proverbs 15:8) "The prayer of the upright is

His *delight!*" Isn't that great? The Almighty actually enjoys His blood-bought children talking to Him!

BEGINNINGS

Right from the start of our ministry, in the small Grahamstown Assembly, we made prayer a major part of church life. We had no church hall. We met on Sundays in the local Masonic Temple Hall. Midweek Bible study, prayer meetings, Saturday night youth meetings and all counseling took place in our home. (No wonder Merle and I were exhausted after 42 months, and actually *asked* for a transfer, in spite of being in a very happy congregation!)

In addition to the regular prayer meeting, we would have seasons of lunchtime sessions in our living room. Students from Rhodes University and the Teachers' Training College would skip lunch, walk to our house and there spend a good hour seeking the Lord, calling on Him to move on the campuses, and in the city. These lunchtime fasting-prayer sessions usually went on for one week at a time. But, on at least one occasion, by popular demand, it was extended for another week.

From time-to-time we also staged a half-night of prayer. A stand-out memory for me was this: Around midnight, when we were winding up the prayer-time, I, and a few students, would walk to the all-night bakery, knock on the locked door to the kitchen, and buy a loaf or two of hot, really hot bread, straight out of the oven. Man, it was delicious! We would tear pieces out of the loaf on the way back to the house and eat the bread on the move. No need for butter, it was moist and fresh just as it was!

I must add, Grahamstown had a 9:00 P.M. curfew, so we walked quietly, we did not want to rouse anybody and be arrested! The risk was worth it, though. At midnight, with Jesus plus hot, freshly baked bread, who needs anything else?

We continued cultivating this "culture of prayer" when we moved to Cape Town, as well as in most other Assemblies through the years. I say "in most," because not every congregation saw the need for special seasons of prayer. In a few instances, it seemed the folk felt the regular weekly prayer meeting was sufficient. So, we did pray, but when we experienced greater growth, it was always associated with greater prayer output.

A GREAT PRAYER WARRIOR

Me? No! Of course, I talk to the Lord almost constantly. But, when it comes to really laying hold of God to move powerfully in a situation, I need others beside me, seeking the Lord together with me, in unity of heart and mind. There is something unleashed in corporate prayer that doesn't happen when praying on ones own.

The Early Church was birthed by and in the Holy Spirit as the disciples prayed together. (Acts 2) When threatened by the authorities the believers met and called on the Lord together. The Spirit empowered them, they preached boldly, and the church continued to grow. (Acts 4) When Peter was imprisoned awaiting execution, the church prayed together. The Lord sent an angel and Peter was miraculously delivered. (Acts 12)

A STAND-OUT MOMENT

I was having a particularly bad time in one Assembly. Several leaders were openly seeking to divide the church and had to be publicly disciplined. This brought strong criticism from some in the congregation who didn't understand the spiritual significance of what was going on. These were nice people, our friends, they argued. How could the church oversight treat them so unlovingly? As the weeks went by, I found myself struggling under quite a weighty depression. So, I took half-a-dozen men away with me for a season of prayer. We called on the Lord to break into the situation and bring release and victory. Quite late that night, as we were praying the guys gathered around me, laid hands on me and prayed specifically for my release. Suddenly, one of the men exclaimed, "There, it's gone!" I felt a definite release, as if a weight was lifted off me. It marked the beginning of a turnaround both for me and for the church. Though not immediately, over time five of the seven who were disciplined returned to apologize. Surely, this was the working of God in response to prayer!

Merle and I came to Schenectady, New York, about two years after Delray and Lorenzo had stepped into the leadership role. By that time the wounded congregation was already on the mend, now numbering about 120 on Sundays. Lorenzo and I made a point of praying regularly, specifically for God to make us a resource center for the Gospel. As time passed, others prayed as well, and now, 11 years in, we have about 700 in attendance on Sunday mornings, excluding children and youth. Though not a large congregation by American standards, we are involved in countries, preaching, teaching, and ministering to children and supporting widows and orphans. In short, we've become a resource center!

Would you like to know which countries? I'll tell you anyway! Mexico, Bulgaria, South Africa, Malawi, Uganda, India, Bangladesh, and Brazil. We also pop in regularly to a South African church-plant in England to give ministry to a growing congregation there. It's my privilege to be personally involved in four of those countries: South Africa, Malawi, India and Mexico. I also visit England on my way to India every year. We also have a very effective and growing outreach to our "Jerusalem," the Schenectady inner city with its broken families, drug addicts and violent-crime lifestyle.

66

Back in the 90's, I attended three successive Prayer Conferences in Jerusalem. Praying in the company of men like Lance Lambert and Johan Facius really brought me great benefit. They taught and demonstrated the principle of *persevering* in prayer, using the acrostic: Pray-Until-Something-Happens! (P.U.S.H.) That has stayed with me throughout the ensuing years. This principle, I hope, will mark my prayer life as long as the Lord gives me strength to serve Him. Don't quit, P.U.S.H.! My strategy, Preach the *word*, pray fervently.

LOVE THE PEOPLE

This in itself is testimony to God's grace in my life. Here's why I say that.

Before conversion, I was quite a private person. During my preteen years, I had no friends, and didn't really miss them. After school, I read books, played records, helped herd my dads few cows, and daydreamed a lot. In my teens, I found friends who lived in the neighborhood, five of them, to be precise, and all of them older than I was. Our common love of cricket and Saturday night movies drew us together. To give you an understanding of how I viewed people in general: if one of the gang brought along another guy on any given outing, I was put out. Why do we have to have this "outsider" horning in on our company? was my reaction.

It was this very "people-issue" that the Lord used

to bring me assurance that I had been truly saved. Before conversion, when I went to church with my ex-drunk brother Joe, I tried to avoid any meaning-ful contact with the young men in the Assembly. They were just "not my type." What's more, in our brief encounters, they would sometimes ask: "Are you saved yet, Noel?"

After surrendering to Christ, I had an up-and-down experience for a while. "Am I saved? Yes, I am. Perhaps I am. No, I don't think I'm saved!" This was the mental war that plagued me until, in my now regular Bible reading, I came across a verse that brought me absolute assurance. It's found in 1 John 3, the 14th verse, and it states: "We *know* that we have passed from death to life because we *love* the *brethren*." I realized then the change that had come over me.

Whereas, before Christ I tried to avoid the fellers in the Assembly, now I was seeking them out. No, naturally speaking they were still not my type. But, would you believe, I wanted to be in their company! I enjoyed being with them and hearing them talk about Christ. What's more, I was not afraid to ask them questions about the faith, and often found their answers very pertinent to my circumstances.

This, in retrospect, is true Christian fellowship. It wasn't just "hanging out" with only a social time in view. It was social, but there was an easy mix of spiritual aspects in the socializing, and I always came away from these informal encounters feeling

I had been enlightened and strengthened in my walk with the Lord.

Of course, the verse I quoted above has a much deeper meaning for us than what I have described. Nevertheless it was the Word the Lord used to give assurance to me that I was truly born again, made new. I loved the brethren, even though they were "not my type!" I had been *Surprised by Grace!* Grace had changed me.

This love for the Brethren, the people of God, is not a sentimental feeling. I can only describe it as a Divinely implanted concern for Christians, a concern that makes one care for their well being, their spiritual growth. It doesn't need the words "I love you" to be spoken. In fact, I use those three words very sparingly. Why? you ask. Because love is so devalued these days. Pop star celebrities shout out to their audience of 30,000 "I love you" and the crowd goes wild, notwithstanding the fact that said celebrity has never met 90-something percent of them, or more!

No, we love as John the apostle commands us, in deed and in truth. We show a sincere, personal interest in God's people, a genuine concern for both their spiritual and natural welfare. When we ask "How are you" we really want to know how they are. We want to contribute to their spiritual growth. They know that they don't just make up the numbers on the church membership register.

Of course, loving God's people means that

sometimes correction and even stern rebuke must be given. "Whom the Lord *loves* He *chastens*," we read in Hebrews 12:6. In His love for us, He disciplines us when we need it, to keep us on the right track. So, it is with us, particularly as leaders. Paul told Timothy to "rebuke, reprove and exhort." True love has to be tough love sometimes. Ask any loving, wise parent! I have found that, in most cases, when the person knows we love them, they receive correction in the right spirit.

Years ago, I became vexed by the foolish behavior of one of our young ladies. In a moment of unrestrained frustration, I called her aside and said "You must cut out this childish behavior. It's absolutely foolish, it's unChristlike and quite unacceptable. Stop it!" with that, I sent her off. The next few days were difficult for me. I thought: "You were too harsh. She's leaving the church because you've hurt her feelings." She appeared at our next meeting, gave me a hug and said: "Thank you for the rebuke. I needed it!" That girl is now a very loyal wife and mother of several children and she has a very steady testimony of godliness.

Another lady was speaking ill of her husband in a home meeting. An elder and I spoke strongly to her about it, and told her it must stop. Within a few days she came and thanked us, and to my knowledge, never criticized her husband in public again. In both cases, these folk knew we loved them, so when correction-time came (after the initial shock!)

they received it and were the better for it.

Unfortunately, this is not true of everyone. I had an occasion to approach a certain man to talk to him about his bad attitude regarding his particular responsibility in the church. Well, he literally erupted! For quite a while I couldn't finish a sentence because he kept interrupting me with angry denials and accusations. Eventually, I said, "Your attitude is decidedly unChristlike, you don't belong in this ministry because of this." He left the church in anger, in spite of approaches by the leadership to meet together and talk the matter out as Christians.

Contrast that with the reaction of a young man whom we had to see in connection with some unwise statements he made publicly. Although, initially it was hard for him, he received our reproof with humility, and is going on well in his particular task for God.

You know, we all have to be ready to receive correction from time-to-time to keep us on track for the Lord. Proverbs 12:1 puts it bluntly: "He who loves instruction loves knowledge. But, he who hates correction is *stupid!*" Generally, if the people know we love them by our track record of care and concern, they will respond well.

One more thing I have learned about ministering correction, it's important to follow up with affirmation. Within a day or two, you can follow up by saying something like this: "I appreciate that you listened the way you did, we value you as a brother" (or fellow laborer, or sister). That's why we felt we had to address this issue. Usually, this helps to smooth things over, and consolidate our relationship in the Lord.

ON THE RECEIVING END OF LOVE

The Love I speak of hasn't been all one-way. Over the years, Merle and I have experienced the love of God through His people in many ways. Here are a few *standout* cases.

In the early days in our first Assembly, as already mentioned, just about all our ministry took place in and from our house. This of course involved us in providing lots of tea, coffee and snacks. It involved extra meals because people, students in particular, would arrive at family mealtimes and we didn't ever want to turn anyone away. Two of the more senior students and a lecturer, members of the Assembly, noticed this, and clubbed together to give us some cash as a regular supplement to our modest monthly salary. This underlined for us the principle Jesus set forth: "Give, and it shall be given to you. . ." We were giving, and we received help without asking, testimony to God's faithfulness and the practical expression of His love through His three disciples.

When we first arrived in Cape Town, our situation was only slightly better than it had been in Grahamstown. Here we had a fairly large church building, but the secretaries office was in our house, and guess where the house was? Right next door to the church! Thus, the phones were going incessantly, and people would often call in at the office, our house, for various (good) reasons, at *all* hours! In addition to my church office, we had two phones and three incoming lines in our house, with no answering machines or voicemail in those days! You can imagine the pressure on us as a couple. It was very difficult to have some regular private time under these circumstances. We couldn't go away for a whole day either, as we had to fetch our three children from school every afternoon at 2:00 P.M.

After a while, a very dear elderly couple, Alan and Shirley, obviously noticed that I was not coping to well. (Yes, God's grace had given me a love for His people, I still needed spells of privacy.) They approached us with this invitation: "Come to our house on Monday mornings. Use our swimming pool. Tell us *when* you want lunch, and *what* you want for lunch. We will go out as soon as you arrive and leave you in peace. We'll come back and serve you lunch at the appointed time. Then you can go fetch the children when you have to." They did this for us for months, giving us a valued few hours for ourselves every Monday. Merle and I will never forget their thoughtful gesture of love.

Years later, when we were located in Cape Town, two of our elders became concerned about the fact that Merle and I owned no property. Prices were always just out of our reach. These men, between themselves, gave us a part-loan/part-gift for the deposit on a very nice little house in a lovely suburb.

We will always be grateful to them for their "maxi-generous" kindness!

WHAT ABOUT AMERICA?

God's people here in the United States have been no less caring and generous. I will mention just two instances from the many. A certain brother, new to the Assembly, wanted to give me a gift in gratitude for time I had spent ministering to him in a delicate situation. I politely declined his offer, I told him we don't minister to individuals for personal gain. This guy was sneaky! A short time later, in casual conversation he asked: "As a South African, what do you miss most, now that you're living in the United States?" I replied, "Among other things, I really miss my canoe." I explained that I regularly took the boat out onto the Milnerton Lagoon in Cape Town, for a bit of exercise and contemplation. He then changed the subject. (I said he was sneaky, didn't I?)

A short time later, I was giving the Wednesday night Bible study to a crowd of about 80 people. I had just begun teaching when in walked this dear man carrying a brand new 12-foot-long canoe, complete with paddles, detachable seat and a life vest! He brought it right up to the front of the church, set it down at my feet, and walked out! I have since had some special times on the Mohawk River with that canoe. It will always be a gift most cherished.

Here's one more standout expression of God's

love for us. A dear man, a longtime member of CALTAB (Calvary Tabernacle), has appointed himself as my personal driver. He noticed that I don't find my way around too easily on these roads, especially in the wintertime when it snows. So, he stands ready at all times to drive me to a preaching venue, whether near or far. But, the *big* benefit is this: When I fly to South Africa or to India, he drives me to New York City, a three hour trip, to catch my plane, and then drives himself straight back home, a six hour drive in all. When I return from South Africa, my flight arrives at 7:00 A.M. This kind Samaritan gets up at 3:00 A.M. to get there on time for me, in spite of me telling him that he should come later, that I don't mind waiting for him a few hours at the airport.

All this is more impressive when I disclose the dear man's age. He is in his mid-80's! Don't be alarmed! He has been driving all around New York State in the line of his work, for many years. He is still more competent and alert than many drivers half his age! I know, he's been my unofficial, unpaid chauffeur for quite a long time now. He is yet another expression of God's gracious, practical love to me.

I could mention many more. God's people are really quite wonderful, their love is expressed in such practical ways. I think of the people who have given me a home from home in their house every time I visited Johannesburg. Another couple does this when I'm in Cape Town. There's also a couple who ferries me to and from Heathrow Airport and accommodate me in their home in Kent, every time I visit England. This they have been doing for years! Then there's the young lady in South Africa who, together with her parents, have been associated with us for more than 20 years. Whenever I'm in their town, she places her car at my disposal for a couple of weeks while she hitches rides with her mother. Indeed, this is as John described true Christian love, "in deed and in truth."

PECULIAR PEOPLE, AMUSING MOMENTS

If you're a longtime regular Bible reader you will no doubt know that the King James Version describes God's people as "a royal priesthood, a *peculiar* people." The word "peculiar" in the 17th century meant "special" or simply "God's own people," as the New King James Version now translates it. I can't resist the temptation however, to present some standout instances where the Lord's dear, special people came over as very peculiar, in the modern sense of the word!

The East London Assembly of God, Saturday night Breaking of Bread service: Some of the benches were moved into a square to give the sense of gathering around the table and not just looking at the back of heads. A young brother was given a few minutes to share a Word on holiness or sanctification with us. As he went on he became quite passionate and urged us to press on in "scantification." These were the days of the miniskirt, so it may have been a freudian slip, and may well have just passed notice. Problem: my brother Joe, now one of the elders, was sitting directly opposite me. As our eyes met, we both came under a heavy "spirit of laughter!" (I'm trying to spiritualize it—but OK I give up!) We just packed up laughing! Joe's shoulders were shaking, he was wiping his eyes with a handkerchief, and I had buried my head between my knees as my whole body convulsed with silent (or nearly silent) laughter! Neither one of us was able to absorb anything from the ministry that followed. All we could think of was this passionate brother vigorously urging us to pursue "scantification!" (Like their Mom, Mrs. Cromhout's "boys" each had a vivid, colorful imagination!) Through all of this, the speaker was oblivious to the effect of his gaffe. A very dear, peculiar brother in Christ!

Cape Town, Friday night prayer meeting: We had a truly lovable brother in the Lord in our Assembly at the time. He was elderly, not very well educated, but passionately devoted to Jesus. Problem: When he was feeling "down" he would try to get out of his pit of depression by shouting loud "Hallelujahs!" On this particular night we could tell Harry was feeling very low. He began to pray in a subdued voice, "Lord, You know that the whole of Cape Town is sunk in sin and deg-gra—da-shin" pause, then a very loud, "Hallelujah!" Some of the prayers jumped in alarm, and others, including "guess who" dissolved into laughter. The incongruousness of praising the Lord for the degradation of the city was just too much for us! Dear brother Harry is with the Lord now and no longer experiencing "downers." One of God's peculiar, special people! For me, some of the Lord's people are unforgettable because of the "peculiar" things they said, or the peculiar decisions they made.

Like the woman, a member of our church, who came forward one night at a meeting and asked us publicly to pray for her. The reason: "The Lord has led me to chuck my job. Now I need a new one," she announced. What was I to say? I couldn't let a statement like that pass without comment. To blame the Lord for such an irresponsible action was "peculiar." I can't remember exactly what I said to the church, but I know we set the matter straight: We can't go making irresponsible, hasty decisions and blame the Lord for doing so! In such a case, the congregation would now have to support her financially until she found another job! That's *not* the Lord's leading! A devoted but unwise disciple of the Lord—and a peculiar decision! She was teachable, and she did learn from the experience.

UNPLANNED STRATEGY

Through the years, as the Lord has continued to surprise us by His grace, Merle and I have done what flowed naturally. We have given first place to the preaching and teaching of the Word, unapologetically. We have tried to model a life of prayerfulness, and we have endeavored to display God's love to His people, by caring, encouraging and, when necessary, by correcting. After 44 years in the ministry, I have seen or heard nothing to cause me to regret, or try to alter that "strategy!"

CHAPTER 7
PREACHING, AS I HAVE LEARNED IT

I remember vividly the first time I got up to preach in our local church. At our Sunday morning services, members were encouraged from time-to-time to bring a short message to the congregation, before the minister brought the main message. I had just come through the troubled waters of uncertainty about my salvation, and the Scriptures were really *alive* for me! I wanted to share this joy with God's people, but as I have already explained, I was no public speaker, I was even too shy to close in prayer at the conclusion of my choir practice. However, the passage in Acts 3 was burning in my bones, especially the part where Peter says to the lame man: "Silver and gold have I none, but such as I have I give to you." Then he healed the man in Jesus' name. The point I wanted to make was: in Christ we *have* something, we *know* we have it, and we need to *pass it on* to others who needed it. (Good outline, hey?)

When the opportunity arrived, I got to my feet quite purposefully and began to read Acts 3, from verse 1. But, a strange thing happened to my voice. It seemed an octave or so higher than usual, and my breathing, I was like a man who had just run a marathon and was struggling to catch his breath after his great exertion! My reading went something like this: Then Peter said [gasp] "Silver and gold [gasp] have I none [gasp]. . ."

Some may have observed at this point, that's not all he's short of, he has no breath either! Somehow I gasped my way through the mini-message, got my point across and collapsed back on the bench were I was sitting. The meeting ran its course, and we all got up and began to move out. No one said a word to me, I was left with my embarrassment and my acute sense of failure. Then as I got to the door a tall fellow in the crowd caught my eye, raised his hand towards me as if in acknowledgment and said, "Thanks, Noel." Just those two words, but they brought relief, and a measure of encouragement. The reason: The guy who uttered them was Dave Kilfoil, a soloist in our music team, and a man of considerable spiritual depth, who also preached from time-to-time. Dave was never given to flattery, and he was always very sparing with his compliments. This was why his two words to me that morning meant so much. Several lessons may be drawn from this cameo.

Here's one: We must be alert for opportunities to speak a simple word to encourage people, one never knows how needed such a word might be at a given moment. Dave's words spurred me on to speak again, and again, with gradually increasing confidence. I also ceased being a heavy breather!

Here's another: We must not use extravagant words, which only amount to flattery. This won't help the person at all. If they have any discernment, they will know their talk, or song, was not "awesome" or "great," as you said it was. So, you will not have helped to spur them on to better things. Worse still, they may *believe* that their moderate performance was indeed "awesome," or "great," because you said so! Thus, their last state shall be worse than their first! You will have given them a false picture of their abilities. Just two words were spoken. I did not need more than these, "Thanks, Noel." Thanks, Dave!

ASPIRATIONS

After a while the local minister and the elders, recognizing a call of God on my life, encouraged me to take a correspondence course in theology as a start. The course included books on preaching, which I read eagerly and sought to apply in the short messages I was allowed to present to the Assembly from time-to-time. I was particularly impressed by a simple outline presented by one of the authors in the course. The writer set forth three points for every good sermon:

Tell them what you are going to tell them.
Then,
Tell them.
Then,
Tell them what you have told them.

Right from the outset, I sought to structure most of my preaching on this pattern:

- Tell them what you are going to tell them: Introduce your subject.
- Tell them: Speak the body of your message.
- Tell them what you have told them: Recap in summary.

One more point is needed, an essential point: Application. This is where I have sometimes fallen short, even to this day. No matter how good your message may be, unless there is a strong, clear challenge to apply the truths presented, the message is reduced to just an interesting "talk." The people may be well informed, but do not necessarily become *transformed* by the Word. This is, after all, the purpose of all preaching, a call to action, a response to the particular Truth that has been presented. The goal: to grow increasingly, progressively into Christlikeness, in character and in behavior. Here are some Scriptures that verify what I've said.

- 1 Peter 2:2 "Like newborn babes, desire the sincere milk of the Word that you may grow thereby."
- Colossians 1:28 "Him [Christ] we proclaim, warning every man and teaching every man

that we may present every man perfect [mature] in Christ."

- 2 Timothy 3:16-17 "That the man of God may become mature, thoroughly equipped for every good work."

These two verses may be summarized thus: The Scriptures are to do two things: they teach us to *believe* right, and to *live* right. The goal is verse 17: Preaching that does not aim to accomplish this falls far short of God's purpose for the preacher.

THE DEVALUING OF PREACHING

These days one sometimes hears Christians saying: "People today don't like to be preached at. They resent anyone making authoritative statements. We should rather just *share* the Scriptures, this is more productive." Certainly we must *share* the Word with people whenever opportunity does so occur. But, regardless of what people *want*, we must give them what GOD wants them to hear. He has commanded His followers to *preach* the Gospel to all creation. This means we are to *proclaim* the message, with authority, as a herald would call citizens together and proclaim the message that had been entrusted to him by the Governor or the King.

After His resurrection, Jesus stated that "repentance and remission of sins should be preached in His Name to all nations. . ." His disciples preached the Word of God everywhere, both to Jews who had the Bible, and to Gentiles who did not have the Bible. The Church grew!

For me, the most compelling passage about preaching is found in Paul's 2nd letter to Timothy. Just listen to this weighty command! "I charge you, therefore, before God and the Lord Jesus Christ Who will judge the living and the dead at His appearing and His kingdom." (*This is serious!*) Preach the Word! Be ready in season (*when convenient*) and out of season (*when not convenient*). (2 Timothy 4:1-2)

No hint here of a time to come when it won't be effective, or necessary to proclaim God's message because of cultural trends and preferences. In fact, the apostle goes on to say: "The time will come when they will not endure sound doctrine." People will not welcome the truth of the Scriptures. He does not tell the young minister to back off and "just share." Rather, he has already commanded him to keep on proclaiming the Word, regardless of the fact that audiences with "itching ears" will turn away from the truth and embrace fables. If you want to show someone how badly a stick is bent out of shape, lay a straight stick next to it. If you want to show how badly our world and everyone in it is "bent out of shape" by sin, lay the straight stick of God's Word alongside the crooked stick of worldly, sin-infected values.

If you want to see people straighten out their lives, proclaim God's grace and forgiveness through The Cross of Christ. Let's preach it with love, with passion and boldness, in the authority of the Holy

Spirit, who Himself has inspired those Scriptures! In spite of the cultural aversion to "preaching," people are still coming to our churches to hear the proclamation of the Word, they are being converted by God's grace and power, and they are growing spiritually under the ongoing teaching and preaching of the Word.

Seekers today are still receiving the Word as the Thessalonian converts did. Paul writes to them: "When you received the Word of God, you welcomed it, not as the word of men, but as it is in truth, the Word of God which also effectively works in you who believe." (1 Thessalonians 2:13)

In my own ministry I always pray for three things: authority, clarity and wisdom. If I don't have the anointing of the Spirit for authority, then my message will merely be interesting. If I don't speak with clarity, then my message will be unintelligible. If I don't apply the message with wisdom, then the hearers won't know what to do with it, it has been largely irrelevant.

SUCH A WEAK, UNWORTHY SERVANT

Often one feels like that: "I am totally inadequate for this great task of proclaiming and teaching God's wonderful life-changing truths." Aren't we all! But, then we remember, "We have this treasure in earthen vessels . . . in jars of clay, that the excellence of the power might be not of us, but of God."

(2 Corinthians 4:7)

The jar might well be a bit scratched, or small, it may be slightly out of shape. The treasure! God's Spirit *in* us, nothing imperfect in Him, right? Here we are again, Surprised by Grace! The Christian ministry is not the treasure without the jar, it is the treasure *and* the jar, *in* the earthen vessel! A lovely description of this ministry is "Truth through Personality." God in His grace takes you, infuses you with His Spirit, and gives you the great honour of being His spokesperson. He channels His Truth through your personality!

Thus, we have Peter, a rough, somewhat unpolished jar, we have Paul, a very well polished, highly educated jar. Both were great servants of God. Thus there is a place for me, a very frail, ill-formed, unimpressive jar, but God placed the treasure in me too! Surprising grace indeed! I identify strongly with these remarks by Cotton Mather, a noted minister of long ago. "The office of the Christian ministry, rightly understood, is the most honourable and important that any man in the whole world can ever sustain, and it will be one of the wonders and employments of eternity, to consider the reasons why the wisdom and goodness of God assigned this office to imperfect and guilty man! The great design and intention of the office of a Christian preacher is to restore the Throne and Dominion of God in the souls of men, to display in the most lively colors, and proclaim in the clearest language the wonderful perfections, offices and grace of the Son of God, and to attract the souls of men into everlasting friendship with Him." My sentiments exactly!

Always climbing higher! Lion's Head, Cape Town, 2011

Perseverance pays off! Made it to the top, with son Mark!

Hyderabad, India

Ministering in Malawi

Celebrating our 50th Wedding Anniversary,
December 2011.

CHAPTER 8

MY FAVORITE BIBLE TOPICS

⎯⎯⎯⎯ ✿ ⎯⎯⎯⎯

The entire Bible is full of fascinating subjects written down by men who were inspired by God to do so. There are some that are especially dear to me. These have significantly impacted my life, and as I have taught on them, they have inspired others also. My top-of-the-list Bible topic is this one: Seeing Christ in the Old Testament. We must note: Jesus Himself claimed to be the subject of the Old Covenant Scriptures. He told the hostile Jews who wanted to kill Him for healing a man on the Sabbath: "If you believed Moses, you would believe Me, for he wrote about Me." Moses is credited with authorship of the first five books of the Bible.

On Resurrection Sunday, He appeared, as yet unrecognized, to the two on the Emmaus road. As they shared their distress with this Stranger about the crucifixion of their Master, He expounded to them "in all the Scriptures the things concerning Himself" remember, the Scriptures to which He referred were what we call the Old Testament, the New was not yet written. A few hours after this, the scene shifts to Jerusalem. The disciples met together in a locked room, for fear of the Jews. Suddenly, the risen Christ appears to them and confers His peace on the frightened group. He shows them His wounds, eats a piece of broiled fish to prove He was not a ghost, and then says: "These are the words I spoke to you while I was still with you, that all things must be fulfilled which were written in The Law of Moses, the Prophets and the Psalms concerning Me." The Law of Moses (the first five Books of the Bible), the Prophets and the Psalms. This is the three-fold division of the Jewish Bible, and covers the entire Old Testament. Therefore, on the authority of Jesus we can search the Old Testament for pictures and references pointing to Him who was yet to come into the world to save us. Here's just a sample.

AT HUMANITY'S GROUND ZERO

On that dreadful day when Adam and Eve ate of the forbidden fruit and fractured Man's relationship with God, the Lord made known His plan to restore that relationship. The Seed (offspring) of the woman, He said, was going to crush the head of the serpent, (the one who successfully tempted Eve) while in the conflict, the serpent would bruise his heel. Do you notice anything unusual in this statement? Reference to the woman's Seed is remarkable. In reproduction, it is the seed of the man that fertilizes the woman's womb. But, here already we have reference to the Virgin birth. God's Champion would be conceived and born without the agency of a man. Centuries later, Paul writes to the Galatians, "When the time had fully come God sent His Son, born of a woman, born under the Law, that He might redeem us. . ."

Three truths about Christ are set forth here in this verse: The Savior was God's Son, no man involved, born of a woman, He was truly human, "the Word was made *flesh* and dwelt among us." Born under the Law, Jesus was born a Jew of the tribe of Judah, a descendant of Abraham and King David. "Moses wrote of Me," said Jesus. Right there at mankind's disaster spot, our Ground Zero, God stated His intention to send the Champion to defeat Satan and bring us back to God. The same chapter, Genesis 3, gives us a beautiful picture of the salvation Christ would bring to sinners.

When Adam and Eve had sinned they became ashamed of their nakedness. So, they sewed fig leaves together and made coverings for themselves. I wonder what these garments looked like? Maybe Eve made the first miniskirt. I'll bet Adam thought it was cute! Perhaps Adam made for himself a pair of baggy pants and a T-(leaf) shirt. Tea-leaf, get it? Or maybe his outfit was a kind of fig-leaf tracksuit, loose-fitting for easy movement. I don't know, but use your imagination! So, the erring pair felt a little more at ease, their nakedness now concealed. A few verses in Genesis 3 we read: "The Lord God made coats of skin for Adam and Eve and clothed them." Right there in the Book of Beginnings, God shows us that our attempts to deal with our guilt, our shame, are not acceptable. The prophet Isaiah writes, "All our righteousnesses [our good deeds] are as filthy rags in His sight." The New Testament teaches that we are *not* saved by *our* works, but by His grace, through faith.

Where is Jesus in this, you ask? Well, where did God get the skins with which He clothed the guilty pair? Obviously from animals, slain animals. These animals had no part in man's sin, they were innocent. They had to be sacrificed in order to provide a covering for the couple's nakedness, a covering not of their own making, but one which satisfied a holy God.

We see Jesus the innocent, sinless Savior Who gave Himself as the perfect sacrifice on The Cross, so that we sinners could be forgiven and made right with God. "Moses wrote about Me," said Jesus.

CHRIST, ACCORDING TO MOSES

There are several more pictures pointing to Christ, in the writings of Moses. In Genesis 22 He is Abraham's Ram caught in the thicket, and sacrificed *instead* of Isaac. (Romans 5:6, 8)

In Exodus 12 He is the Passover Lamb that was sacrificed so that Israel's firstborn sons would not die when the angel of death passed over Egypt in judgment. (1 Corinthians 5:7-8)

In Exodus 16 He is the Manna that God sent down from heaven to feed the Israelites throughout their 40 years' journey through the wilderness. (John 6:33-35)

In Exodus 17 He is the Rock that Moses struck, that gushed forth water for God's thirsty people to drink. (John 6:37-38; 1 Corinthians 10:1-4)

In Leviticus 16 He is the scapegoat on whom Aaron laid his hands to transfer the sins of Israel, and to symbolically carry them away into the wilderness. (1 John 3:5; John 1:29)

HERE'S ONE MORE FROM MOSES' PEN

In Numbers 21 we read (yet again) of Israel's rebellion against the Lord and His leader Moses. The Lord sent fiery serpents among them, and many of them died of the snake bites. When the people repented and pleaded with Moses to entreat the Lord for forgiveness, the Lord told Moses to make a serpent of bronze or brass, and erect it on a pole, that it may be seen from far off. Everyone who had been bitten could be healed if they would look at it.

Where is Christ in this account? Just two verses before the golden text of the Bible, John 3:16, Jesus states: "As Moses lifted up the serpent in the wilderness, even so must the Son of Man be lifted up, that whoever believes in Him should not perish but have everlasting life." (John 3:14-15)

This tells us that sin is like poison, it affects the whole person, it's lethal. It tells us that there is no cure of human origin. No amount of psychotherapy will do it. Just as the repentant Israelites had to *look*, intently, on God's remedy the upraised serpent, in order to be healed, so you and I have to acknowledge our sins and look in faith to the Savior who was lifted up on The Cross. This is the only way the sin which has poisoned us all, can be removed.

I must emphasize, it's not Jesus' teachings that save us, matchless though they are, it's not His perfect example of love that neutralizes the poison of sin. It is His death on The Cross, the uplifted pole, that deals with it. The Lord used this figure again, just a few days before He was crucified. He said "And I, if I be lifted up from the earth, will draw all peoples to Myself." Then John adds the explanation: "This He said, signifying by what death He would die." (John 12:32-33)

MOSES WROTE OF ME

Israel's lawgiver wrote a whole lot more of the Seed of the woman, the Savior Who was to come. I want to move on in the Old Testament to see what one of the prophets wrote of Him.

CHRIST ACCORDING TO ISAIAH

The prophet Isaiah ministered around the 8th

Century B.C. of all the prophets, he wrote most extensively about the Messiah, the Savior who was to come. He would not only be Israel's Savior, the Gentiles would also come to Him and be saved.

In Isaiah, chapter 7, the prophet writes of the Virgin birth. In chapter 9, the Child to be born would be the Mighty God, the Everlasting Father. His kingdom would be extended universally, extending true peace to the world, the Messiah, without limits. In chapter 11 He would be the Root from the stem of Jesse, David's father, who would stand as a banner to the people, to whom the Gentiles would gather, and whose resting place would be glorious. In chapter 42 He would be God's anointed Servant, the Messiah, who would bring forth justice to the Gentiles. Nothing would cause Him to deviate from the Divine purpose. "He will not fail nor be discouraged till He has established justice in the earth."

THE CLEAREST ADVANCE RECORD

Of all the prophesies in Isaiah's writings, the clearest, most detailed one is in chapter 53. Here the prophet writes of the Servant of the Lord who would be despised, rejected, and punished, not for His own sins, but for the sins of others . . . for us.

On my first visit to Israel in 1975, I visited the Shrine of the Book in Jerusalem. Here I saw copies of the recently discovered Dead Sea Scrolls displayed in glass cabinets. One of my fellow travelers, an

Anglican priest pointed out a striking feature of the scrolls. All had suffered damage to some degree over the centuries. All except one. The 53rd chapter of Isaiah was entirely intact. This scroll was the center feature in the display, a remarkable testimony and witness to our Jewish friends in the Holy City, the clear record of this Servant of God who would be wounded for our, and their transgressions, Who would have all our sins laid upon Him, the innocent One. We pray for the day when the Lord's Old Covenant people will have their spiritual eyes opened that they might see, the Messiah for whom they have been waiting has already come and paid the price for their sins, and will come the second time in power, to tread down His enemies and reign over all the world from His throne in Jerusalem. Then, and only *then*, will there be world peace, when the Prince of Peace reigns on the earth. "And of the increase of His government, and of peace, there will be no end. . ." (Isaiah 9:7)

CHRIST IN THE PSALMS

Jesus claimed that the Psalms made mention of Him. We will look at just two.

- Psalm 22 begins with the despairing cry, "My God, my God, why have You forsaken Me?" These are the very words Jesus uttered in His awful agony when He was crucified. The most striking reference to His suffering comes in verse 16: "They pierced My hands and My feet." David penned this Psalm around 1,000 B.C. At that time, crucifixion, the piercing of hands and feet, was not employed in the land. It was only brought in as a form of execution when the Romans began to rule Israel in 164 B.C. We know also that this never happened to David. How could he describe these details of the Savior's suffering more than 800 years before these events? Answer: the Holy Spirit, who inspired all the writers of the Bible, inspired him to describe the method of torture and death by which the Savior would suffer for our sins.

- Psalm 16 was quoted by the apostle Peter, on the Day of Pentecost, when he preached to the crowd, and 3,000 were converted. Verse 10 reads: "You will not leave My soul in Sheol [the place of the departed] nor will you allow Your Holy One to see corruption." Peter applied this to the death and resurrection of Jesus. Our Lord would not stay dead, His body would not decay in the grave as all corpses do. Again, David is writing of our Lord 1,000 years before the event. Clearly, he was inspired by the Holy Spirit to describe the death and physical, literal resurrection of our Savior.

THE CRUCIAL ISSUE

It's been wonderful for me to find these references to Christ all through the Old Testament. I have selected only a few. Peter, when preaching to the Roman soldier Cornelius, says of Jesus: "To Him gave all the prophets witness." Clearly, our Lord Jesus is the Center of the Bible, in both Old and New Testaments. Here's the issue you and I have to settle.

IS HE THE CENTER OF OUR LIVES?

If you have shifted Him even slightly off center, isn't this a good time to put that right?

CHAPTER 9
THREE STANDOUT PSALMS

————————

At various times any one of the 150 Psalms can speak to me strongly. There are three that stand out for me prominently and consistently. Let me take you through them, one at a time and see if they do something for you.

PSALM ONE

This is sometimes called "The Preface Psalm," because all the others take something from this one and enlarge upon it. The Psalm begins with a blessing on a person who does *not* do certain things.

- vs 1: He does not walk in the counsel of the ungodly. The blessed man doesn't look to unbelievers for advice concerning his path through life. The unbeliever lives in a different kingdom, serves a different god, and generally has a different set of values. The blessed man knows he will not benefit from counsel on life issues from those not surrendered to Christ. Nor does he stand in the way of sinners. He won't station himself alongside the ungodly. He won't be identified with them. He belongs to a different kingdom, the Kingdom of God. "He does not sit in the seat of the scornful." He does not settle down among those who ridicule the things of God. He does not seek their kind of entertainment. He does *not* do such things.

THESE ARE THE THINGS THE BLESSED PERSON DOES

- vs 2: "His delight is in the Law of the Lord." He loves God's Word, His commandments, His precepts. He is like Jeremiah the weeping prophet, who said, "Your Words were found and I did eat them. Your Word was to me the joy and rejoicing of my heart. . ." (Jeremiah 15:16) The evidence of the Psalmist's delight: he meditates in what he reads, day and night. He doesn't only read the Bible as a religious duty. The blessed man thinks deeply about what he reads. He turns it over in his mind, this way, that way, to discover how what he reads can be applied to his life. Meditation of course, goes together with memorization. It's hard to meditate on a Scripture passage if you haven't committed it to memory. For some of us, we wish that verse in Psalm 119 read: "Thy Word have I logged on my computer that I may look it up when I need it!" It doesn't say that! It says: "Thy Word have I hidden in *my heart* that I might not sin against Thee." (Psalm 119:11)

Memorizing Scripture gives a two-fold benefit: It's insurance against falling into sin, and it ensures that you can turn your mind to the relevant passage at any time without going to your "gadget" for help! Do you want to get a good grip on God's Word? Then look at your hand. To grip anything firmly you have to use all five fingers, right? Let's count from the little finger. To get a firm grip on God's Word, you need to *hear* the Word. Next finger, you need to *read* the Word for yourself. Middle finger, you need to *study* the Word. Go to Bible study meetings. Use a Bible dictionary. That's a start. Second, or pointer finger, you need to *memorize* the Word. Start with one verse that speaks to you. Repeat that verse to someone, for practice. Do the same with a second verse, then a third, and so on. But, keep revising the verses you have already done, don't lose them from your memory bank! So, we have a four-fingered grip on the Word. But, that's not firm enough. You need the fifth finger for a really firm grip, the thumb. This answers to *meditation*. The person whom God calls blessed is one whose delight in the Bible is evidenced by regular meditation in the Scriptures. Make sure you have a firm grip on the Word, using all five "fingers." *Hear* it, *read* it, *study* it, *memorize* it, and *meditate* on it.

- vs 3: The Person who does this, says the psalmist, is like a tree planted by rivers of water. No risk of dehydration here! If one stream fails, there are more rivers to sustain the tree. This person will have a productive life, he bears fruit in his season. No Christian wants to be unproductive, we want to be a credit to God. Jesus said: "Herein is My Father glorified, that you bear *much* fruit." The way to the productive life is to delight in the Word, and to meditate in it continuously. Furthermore, the tree is evergreen, its leaf will not wither. This flourishing, fruitful evergreen tree consistently provides man, birds and animals with fruit and shade. Don't you want your life to be like that? Flourishing in all you do, bearing the fruit of Christlikeness, and providing spiritual nourishment and shelter for needy people? That's my desire.

NOW, STARK CONTRAST

- vs 4: "Not so, the wicked!" That is apparently how the original text reads for verse 4. It's emphatic! Far from being likened to a fruitful riverside tree, the ungodly are described as chaff which is separated from the wheat on the threshing floor and tossed to the wind, to be blown away!
- vs 5: "Therefore the wicked will not stand in the judgment, nor sinners in the congregation

of the righteous." There is a great separation coming. Remember the parable Jesus told of the wheat and the tares, or chaff, in which He said the wheat will be gathered into the barn. But, the tares will be gathered into bundles to be burned. Frightening prospect! Let us determine to meet the conditions for the blessed life as set forth in this "Preface" Psalm. Live for Jesus, delight in God's Word, meditate in the Scriptures continually. That way we become like that tree, firmly planted, flourishing, productive and evergreen, having a consistent testimony of the reality of the living Savior. For whatever such a person does, prospers. (vs 3)

- vs 6: "For the Lord knows the way of the righteous." His eye is upon you constantly, to guide you, and to protect you as you walk with Him, day by day.

PSALM 23, THE SHEPHERD PSALM

This Psalm was not only written to comfort the sick and to cheer the mourners at a funeral. Come with me through its six verses and you'll see, it describes different stages of the believer's life as he or she follows Christ.

- vs 1: "The Lord is my Shepherd." That's were we start. None of what follows applies to anyone who is not surrendered to Jesus and living for Him. "He leads me." In the Middle East, the Shepherd generally walks in front of His flock. He decides where they go, where they graze, where they will sleep. They follow Him. We must get rid of the idea, if we have it, that the Lord walks *with* me on life's road, or that He is my partner. No, He is the Leader, I, the follower. As sheep submit to the Shepherd, so you and I are to submit to our Lord. As we do that, He supplies our needs: "I shall not want [for anything]." As Christ followers, we go through different stages. Sometimes, we may even repeat some of these stages. Let's examine them.

THE TRANQUILITY STAGE

- vs 2: "Green pastures, quiet waters." That's *nice* isn't it? All is well, all is peace. My sins are forgiven, my life is in order, because Jesus is in control. He is blessing me abundantly!
- vs 3(a): He is busy restoring my soul. Inner wounds are being healed, the effects of past failures and disappointments are being remedied.

THE RESPONSIBILITY STAGE

- vs 3(b): Here comes a shift. "He leads me in the paths of righteousness for *His name's sake*." Now its not so much about what

Christ does for me, but, what I have to do for Him. "For *His* Name's sake." Now the path becomes quite steep, this path of righteousness. My life must line up straight with His holy standards. My conduct must be in line with His requirements of godliness, even at personal cost. I have a responsibility to be a credit to Him, to live right and do right, even at the cost of personal ease and comfort. The paths of righteousness can often be rocky and steep! But, I keep following the Shepherd, as He keeps leading me.

THE DARK AND GLOOMY STAGE

- vs 4: ". . .the Valley, Shadow, Death. . ." Not a sought-after tourist route! A great preacher once termed this as "the dark night of the soul." It's not the sort of experience after which we seek! But, the Shepherd actually *leads* us in this phase too, just as he leads us in tranquility and up the challenging responsibility phase. This is when we learn to "walk by faith, not by sight." We may not be conscious of His presence, only of darkness and gloom, it's lonely, depressing. We *believe* He is near, for we have His promise: "I will never leave you nor forsake you." (Hebrews 13:5)

I encountered this dark valley early on in my ministry. For days, or was it weeks, I felt spiritually cold, dry, desolate, and this, not for lack of prayer. "God, where are You?" I cried repeatedly. No answer! I got to the place where I said, as I recall: "Lord, I believe You are here, although I have no evidence, no consciousness of Your presence. So, by faith, I will act 'as if' You are here." I will take You at Your Word. You promised that You will never leave me nor forsake me. So, I will take that Word by faith, in spite of how I feel. It took a few days, but finally the gloom gave way to light once more, and I learned a never-to-be-forgotten lesson. We must *not* rely on feelings for our assurance. Take God at His Word. Corrie ten Boom said: "Feelings come and feelings go, and feelings are deceiving. My warrant is the Word of God, none else is worth believing." We must not omit what is, for me, the key word in this verse, the word "through." He leads us *through*, not *into* the dark valley. In the gloom we trust in the guidance and protection of His rod, and His staff.

THEN COMES THE JOY AND CELEBRATION STAGE

- vs 5: "You prepare a table before me in the presence of my enemies." Notice: In this verse the enemies are still around, but here, they do not attack, they are compelled to merely observe the joyous feast, the honour of being freshly anointed, the enjoyment of the over-flowing cup. I wonder, do you identify with this journey I've described? Perhaps you're in the valley phase, and you're wondering what you did wrong that you have landed here! If so, remember, if you have been following the Shepherd, He is leading you, not *into* the valley, but *through* the valley, to the feast on the other side. Keep trusting, even in the dark. He is ever the Good Shepherd and He will take you through.

THE ASSURED DESTINATION

- vs 6: "Surely goodness and mercy shall follow me all the days of my life, and I will dwell in the house of the Lord forever." As we keep following the Shepherd, we have two traveling companions, or bodyguards, actually, Goodness, and Mercy. They follow us through all the stages of our life's journey right up to our final destination, His House, Heaven, our eternal home. All this is because of the Lord, Who gave His life for us, Who is our Good Shepherd, and we uncomplainingly follow His lead.

PSALM 92

This Psalm is a standout one for me, chiefly because of its twin illustrations of the Christian life: the Palm tree, and the Cedar of Lebanon.
- vs 12: "The righteous shall flourish like

a Palm tree. He shall grow like a Cedar in Lebanon."

The Palm tree, tall and stately, with its leaves reaching up towards heaven, has been called the prince of the vegetable world. It can yield up to 100 pounds of coconuts annually, right up until it reaches a hundred years of age. What is so remarkable is that it grows and flourishes in desert places, where other plants cannot survive. Weary desert travelers, sighting an oasis in the distance, are encouraged, they know that soon they will be refreshed by the cool water, their hunger will be satisfied by the fruit of the palm, and they will find rest in its shade. Thus, we as true believers, are like that Palm tree. This world is like a desert, dry, barren, hostile to the Christian life. But, like the Palm tree, we cannot merely survive, but we can grow spiritually and flourish, even in unfavourable conditions.

We are like Enoch, who walked blamelessly with God during the most wicked of times, which led to the Lord sending the Flood to destroy the earth, and to start afresh with Noah. We can be like Daniel who served the Lord faithfully, in Babylon of all places, for at least 70 years. Even his enemies, in trying to dig up "dirt" to discredit him, confessed: "We will not find anything against this Daniel. . ." His was a blameless life, flourishing in pagan Babylon, bearing fruit for the Lord, exerting a godly influence on kings.

"They shall flourish like the Palm tree." How does this happen? The roots of this desert monarch go down deep beneath the surface and tap into the underground springs. What is the lesson for us? Our spiritual roots, the invisible part of our life, must go deep into Christ, into His Word. That part of my life which is hidden, not my public life, not my preaching, but my secret, private times with the Lord in prayer, in the Scriptures, in meditation . . . this ensures that I flourish in the desert of this hostile world. "They shall *grow* like the Cedar in Lebanon." The Palm tree grows in the desert, the Cedar grows on Lebanon's mountains. It is exposed to wind, storm, rain, blizzards, and it still *grows*!

Here we have an illustration of the Christian who does not live a sheltered life, but who is exposed to tests, trials, and persecutions, who comes through standing tall and strong, through the grace of God. It represents the believer who is "strengthened with power by His Spirit in the inner man. . ." (Ephesians 3:16)

It describes the believer who has experienced what James writes about: "Count it all joy . . . when you have various trials, knowing that the testing of your faith produces patience [perseverance]. But, let patience have its perfect work, that you may be perfect and complete, lacking nothing." (James 1:2-4)

Here's a striking bit of info: cedars from Lebanon were used in the building of Solomon's Temple. If we endure the tests and storms of life, we can grow strong in Christ and become God's building material for His temple, the Church of Jesus Christ. I want that for my life, don't you? "The righteous shall *flourish. . .*" we are not aiming merely for survival! "They shall *grow. . .*" we don't insist on a comfortable Christian life. Nice if that happens! But, we are prepared to face the storms that come our way with a robust faith, and grow strong, that He may use us to build up His church, His kingdom. Then, verse 14 applies: "They shall still bear fruit in old age. They shall be fresh and flourishing, to declare that the Lord is upright. . ." As we flourish and grow, the Lord gets the credit! And rightly so!

CHAPTER 10
STANDOUT BIBLE HEROES

—❧•❧—

The Bible records the lives and exploits of many heroic figures: Moses, Joshua, Elijah, Paul, to name just a few. I want to talk about three of these heroes whose lives stand out quite markedly for me.

FIRST-CALEB

The Lord said of him: ". . .My servant Caleb . . . as a different spirit in him and has followed Me fully . . ." (Numbers 14:24) This man so impressed me that I named our first Dalmatian puppy (a gift from friends) after him. He lived for 17 years and gave us much pleasure and also protection, before we had to euthanize him because of old age. (The dog, not the man!)

Now, Caleb (The man, not the dog!) was one of the 12 spies Moses sent across the Jordan to check out the Promised Land. He and Joshua came back with a "let's go get it" report. "It's a good land," they said, "flowing with milk and honey." With the Lord's help we will take possession of it!

The other 10 spies however, instilled fear into

the people with their negative report. They told of the fortified cities and the giants, and stated in effect that Israel would be no match for the Canaanites. Tragically, the people went along with the majority report. In His anger at their unbelief, God consigned them to wander around in the wilderness for the next 38 to 39 years, until that generation, excepting Caleb and Joshua, had died out. Caleb had to wait for over 40 years to take possession of his inheritance, because of the unbelief of his brethren. Through all of that time he showed that he indeed had a different spirit to that of his fellows.

This is evidenced by: his unselfish loyalty. He didn't allow his disappointment to embitter him. Caleb didn't arrange a private crossing for himself into the promised land. He stayed with his people through their wilderness journeys. After the nation crossed the Jordan, he campaigned together with them for at least five years, helping the others to drive out the enemy and take possession of their portion of land.

How do you react when friends disappoint you, and spoil things for you, with bitterness? I pray that in such instances, I will display a different spirit, as Caleb did. Don't you? His consistent, unwavering faith and courage.

After five years of the campaign in Canaan, he says to Joshua: "The Lord has kept me alive these 45 years . . . and now here I am this day, 85 years old. As yet, I am as strong this day as on that day when Moses sent me . . . Now therefore, give me this mountain!" ". . .It may be that the Lord will be with me and I shall be able to drive them out, as the Lord said." (Joshua 14:10-12 SELECTED)

"This mountain" that he wanted was the very territory of the giants that had put fear into the hearts of the unbelieving 10 spies, 45 years previously! They feared the obstacles, and forgot God's promise. Caleb had a different spirit. He remembered the promise and tackled the obstacles in faith, conquering the giants and taking possession of the fertile territory of Hebron. (Joshua 14:13-14)

How do you respond in such situations? In most cases, when opportunities present themselves, obstacles are also present. The spies brought back grapes, and reports of giants. The 10 focused on the giants, Joshua and Caleb focused on the grapes. The apostle Paul wrote to the Corinthian church: "A door of opportunity [for the Gospel] is open to me, *and* there are many *adversaries*." (1 Corinthians 16:9)

Opportunities, adversaries, grapes and giants: which wins the day for you? May we always display a different spirit from that of the negative, fearful, unbelieving majority. May we display the heroic, consistent, enduring faith and courage that Caleb displayed through all those 45 years. For His God, the God who helped Him, is our God too!

MY SECOND STANDOUT HERO IS ACTUALLY A HEROINE-RUTH

Yes, I know! These days it's not politically correct to "feminize" the word, it's "hero," whether male or female. I prefer the word that distinguishes a female from a male. Notice, I say, "distinguishes." To do so does not discriminate, it merely identifies the gender of the person concerned, a truly heroic, honourable woman.

If you have read the book of Ruth, the 8th book in our Bible, you may have noticed, at least six times, she is identified as being a Moabitess, and once, that she is a foreigner. This, I believe, is to underline the fact that, under the Old Covenant she was excluded from the benefits of the covenant, from God's promises, and from even entering into a place of worship with the Israelites. She was a Gentile, excluded from the blessings enjoyed by the Lord's People. Added to that, Moabites were expressly forbidden to worship with Israel because of the harm they did to that nation, during their wilderness journeys.

See the odds stacked against this young widow? Yet, in the record of the genealogies of Jesus, Ruth the Moabitess is listed as the great grandmother of King David, and therefore one of the human channels of our salvation. Christ was born of the line of David, through Ruth's line! (Matthew 1:1-16)

Here we see a foreshadowing of the saving grace of God. We Gentiles, strangers from the covenants of God, are saved and brought into God's family by His grace, through faith in the Messiah, our Lord Jesus Christ, and we become the spiritual channels of that saving grace to our lost world.

RUTH'S 3-POINT EXAMPLE

This young widow displays three features that you and I ought to emulate.

- Her unconditional commitment to Naomi her mother-in-law, and to Naomi's God, the God of Israel. "Wherever you go, I will go. Wherever you lodge, I will lodge. Your people shall be my people, and your God, my God." (Ruth 1:16)

We must understand, Ruth, widowed by the death of her husband, Naomi's son, was turning her back on her family, her parental home, her people and her gods, to follow Naomi to a land she had never seen, to face a future which was decidedly uncertain. Widows in those days had no Pension Funds, no Social Security, no Food Stamps. Their only hope was for relatives to provide for them or to find a husband to care for them. This is what makes Ruth's commitment to Naomi and to the true God so heroic. Win or lose, she was committed! I find this very challenging, don't you? We should ask ourselves, how strong is our commitment to Christ and to His people, the church?

Her Moabite sister-in-law Orpah, also a widow,

faced the same decision. When Naomi was leaving Moab, both girls wept. While Ruth clung to Naomi and the Lord, Orpah went back to Moab, to her false gods and to her old life. Orpah is a type of so many today, who are greatly moved by the challenge to follow Jesus. They even weep at altar calls, but they don't follow through. Rather than turning their backs on the old life of sin, they go back to it! I have learned over the years not to be too impressed by an emotional confession of the need for Jesus, too often such a commitment is shallow, and not lasting. It is Orpah all over again, tears, but no turning, no repentance! Ruth, by contrast, wept, turned her back on the old life and embarked on a new life with God's people. Her very moving words of commitment to Naomi and the God of Israel were followed through by her actions.

- The second notable feature in Ruth's life was her humble servant attitude.

It is evident that she was quite an attractive young woman. She could have strolled around the village and attracted any number of young men, if she so desired. But, her priority was to put food on the table for her mother-in-law and herself. So, she goes into the harvest fields to glean among the reapers.

This needs some cultural and historical explanation. The Lord had commanded His people to care for the poor in this manner. At harvest time, by agreement with the landowner, a poor person could follow close behind the reapers and scrape together the grains of wheat that spilled over and fell to the ground in the reaping process. This amounted to hard work for small gains, but, at least the poor could have food without having to beg for it.

This attractive young woman humbled herself, bending down and scraping together the grains for hours each day, so that she could provide some food for Naomi and herself. No pampered beauty, she displayed a servant heart, one which you and I, servants of Jesus, ought to imitate. Whether we are full-time ministers or "laypersons," we are called to be servants, not celebrities! This is a good point at which to pose the question: when last have you "bent low" to *serve* someone, in Jesus' Name?

• Her third notable feature, Her Perseverance.

The last verse of the second chapter of Ruth records: ". . .She stayed close by the young women of Boaz to glean until the end of barley harvest and wheat harvest. . ." How long would that be, you ask? Just about three months! That's six days a week, for about 10 to 12 weeks, from sunup to sundown, with a short break during the heat of the day!

That, for me, is a powerful illustration of perseverance, don't you agree? It's a powerful challenge for us to "keep on keepin on," as they say in the deep South! In God's kingdom there are no rewards for faders and quitters. In Galatians 6 we read: "Don't get tired of doing what is good. Don't get discouraged and give up, for we will reap a harvest of blessing at the appropriate time." (NLT)

THE BIG QUESTION

"But," you ask, how did Ruth become one of the forbearers of our Savior, since she wasn't an Israelite to begin with? The Answer: Boaz! This wealthy Jewish landowner fulfilled the duty of the Kinsman Redeemer (Levirate Law) by marrying her.

This is how it worked. God decreed that, should an Israelite man die childless, a near relative was to marry his widow. The child born of that marriage would be reckoned as the deceased husband's child. Thus, the family name would be perpetuated, and the land of the deceased would be redeemed for the widow.

One night during harvest, at Naomi's instigation, Ruth snuck into where Boaz lay sleeping, and lay down at his feet. (Let's fervently pray that Hollywood never decides to make a movie of the story of Ruth, you can imagine what they would do with this incident!)

The plain fact is, Ruth and Boaz are the epitome of godliness and purity, in the midst of the immorality and godlessness that characterized the time of the Judges. Read Judges, and see for yourself!

Back to the barn! Sometime during that night Boaz becomes conscious of the alarming fact, "there is a *woman* lying at my feet!" Now follows the most moving point of the whole story. Ruth identifies herself, "I am Ruth, your maidservant." Then, she appeals to him, "Spread the corner of your garment over me, for you are my nearest kinsman." In making this appeal, she is asking him to take her under his wing, as husband, as protector, and as provider, in accordance with the Levirate Law already referred to. There were some details to deal with but, in brief, Boaz graciously, and I think, gratefully, marries her. All the evidence shows that he really *did* fancy her, anyhow! Read the Book for yourself and see! Their first child, a boy, was named Obed, who became David's grandfather. That is how the Moabite woman was brought into the Covenant nation, and became a human channel of God's salvation to the world.

In marrying Ruth, Boaz becomes a type of Christ, our Redeemer. We too, are spiritually destitute, without hope in the world. God's Son became a human being, our relative, so that He could "spread His garment over us," if we appeal to Him. As Ruth, and Naomi, were rescued from a life of hopelessness and poverty by Boazs' action, so you and I are rescued from our hopeless, lost estate, by Christ's Redemption through The Cross.

Our heroine, whose name means "friend," stands out for me, because of her unconditional commitment to God and to His people, because of her humble servant attitude, and because of her dogged perseverance. See how God rewarded her! Let us ensure that our lives display these same three features she displayed. As Ruth became one of the physical channels of salvation to the world, so you and I can become the spiritual vehicles of salvation, through our testimony of Christ our Savior.

THIRD-DANIEL

In 605 B.C., the Babylonians conducted their first major raid on Judah and took away captive some choice young men, with the object of educating and training them to put them to work in the growing Babylonian kingdom. Daniel and his three friends were among the captives.

Daniel (God is my Judge) stands out as a true hero for the following reasons. When offered food that he knew had been offered to idols, Daniel refused to eat it, or to drink their wine. Instead he appealed to the chief officer that he be permitted to eat only vegetables, and drink only water. We must understand—this was not merely a case of "May I see what else you have on the menu?" These young guys were prisoners of war! They had the opportunity of a three-year long education program in the Babylonian university. If they failed to cooperate, they faced two options: one, the dungeon and two, execution. To make matters all the more serious, the king himself had selected their food. In those days, you do *not* cross the king, you were not likely to escape his wrath. What I find all the more admirable is this: Daniel was at this time only a teenager! Some commentators put his age at 14! Yet, he displayed remarkable courage in standing by his convictions. He was not about to compromise his faith and dishonor his God, whatever it may cost him. Just imagine how you would feel in the same circumstances. You have been forcibly removed from your home, your family, your land. You have been transferred several hundred miles away. You now have opportunity to save your skin, get a good education and go to work in this land of your captivity. Oh dear, here comes the food, nonkosher food, dishes that have been offered to idols. What would you do? A small compromise perhaps? Surely, the Lord will understand? Not so for this young hero.

We read: "Daniel *purposed* in his *heart* that he would *not* defile himself with the king's delicacies . . ." (Daniel 1:8) The Lord gave him favour with the official, his request was granted, and after a time, he and his friends turned out a lot healthier than the others who had stuck to the regulation food. Centuries earlier the Lord had said to Samuel: "Them that honor Me, I will also honor."

Second outstanding feature: Daniel's uncompromising integrity.

The years are passing. God's favour and Daniel's hard work have brought him promotion after promotion. This arouses the envy and jealousy of his colleagues. They set about trying to dig up some dirt with regard to Daniel, but their efforts are unsuccessful. Now note their testimony of his life and conduct: "We shall not find any charge against this Daniel, unless we find against him concerning his God." (Daniel 6:5)

What a testimony, especially as it comes not from his friends, but from his enemies! I wonder how you and I would shape up here? Can our workmates give such a ringing testimony of us in the workplace? As Christ followers we are urged to be "blameless and harmless, children without fault in the midst of a crooked and perverse generation, among whom you shine as lights in the world." (Philippians 2:15) With the Daniel-kind of resolve in our hearts, God will enable us to be those lights in our spiritually and morally dark world, our "Babylon."

Daniel's courageous conviction, his integrity, and 3rdly, his *Consistent Prayer Life*.

When his enemies couldn't find any dirt concerning Daniel, they tricked the king into signing a decree that forbade anyone from petitioning any god or man for 30 days. A person who transgressed would be fed to the lions. When it became known to Daniel, we read that he went home, opened his windows towards Jerusalem and "knelt down on his knees three times that day." Now here's my main point, "*As he had always done!*" (Daniel 6:10)

Daniel's prayer life wasn't just his *spare wheel*, which he pulled out in an emergency, it was his *steering wheel* to guide him on his road every day. I am challenged by this, aren't you? Of course, a spare wheel is a necessary part of your car tools. One needs it if you get a flat tire. So, in life's emergencies, we pull out the spare, we cry to God for assistance, and He comes to our aid. But, every cars *essential* is the steering wheel. We need it constantly, to steer the car with it. So too, our prayer life, it should be as constant as is the steering wheel on our car steering us through every day. Paul writes to the Thessalonians. "Pray without ceasing." Daniel displayed a courageous conviction, an uncompromising integrity, and a consistent prayer life.

Lastly, this hero of faith exercised: God-Glorifying Influence on Others.

Remember His stand as a teenager about the food offered to idols? His three friends were present when that drama was acted out. Some time later, they had to face a huge test. "Bow before the image of gold, or burn in the furnace!" They refused to bow. "Our God whom we serve," they stated, "is able to deliver us." Great faith, right? But, they go even further, "But *if not*, we still won't bow and serve your gods." (Daniel 3:17-18 PARAPHRASED)

Indeed we are to be commenced for faith that says. "God is able to get us out of this mess." It is even more commendable if we say: "Even if *not*, we still won't compromise!" I believe these brave young men were able to stand in the trial because of their friend Daniels' example. His influence stirred them to similar courageous faith. Daniel lived in Babylon throughout the 70 years of Israel's exile. His godly influence extended over decades to five kings. He is the only person in the Bible to have been called by an angelic being, "O Daniel, man greatly beloved." (Daniel 10:11) What a testimony!

Only Jesus had greater approval from heaven.

Indeed, he is a stand-out hero for me among many Bible heroes. May in our lives exhibit his heroic features. May we have the courage to stand by our convictions. May we display impeccable integrity in the workplace. May our prayer life be consistent and not just a spare wheel to be used in emergencies. Finally, may our influence for Christ extend in increasing measure to others who need Him.

CHAPTER 11
CHRIST-ianity or SELF-ianity

———— ❦ ————

An astute observer recently wrote that in the West, the Christian faith has become so "need-centered," Christianity is now better termed SELF-ianity. Instead of theology—the study of God, we now have ME-ology, the study of the Bible with the emphasis on Man and on what God can and should do for us. Of course, this is a generalization, there are blessed exceptions. There are Christ followers who pray "not my will but Thine be done," and who live out their prayer by self sacrifice and genuine submission of heart to the Lordship of Christ. Nevertheless, I see a great need to emphasize and teach what I term certain "crucial doctrines" of the faith so that we remedy this trend toward an anemic Christianity, and get back to the robust version described in the Scriptures, and exhibited at various times in church history. We must be "established in the faith" as Paul states to the believers in Colosse, we must be rooted in Christ, built up in Him, we are to become complete, mature in Him. (Colossians 1:28; 2:5-6)

SO WHERE DO WE START?

We start with the *bad* news—the dreadful sinfulness of the human race. Understanding this truth leads to a heightened appreciation of the *good* news. Rightly understood, it results in a needed shift in focus—from "me" to Christ, from what He will do for me—a good *starting* point—to what He requires me to do for Him, a *maturing* process. Of course, we know the Lord loves sinners, that's why He sent His Son to die for us, that we might have our sins forgiven, and come into a saving, loving relationship with Him. However, it is of extreme importance that we realize how sinful sin is. Sometimes, we seem to merely brush it off by saying, "Well I'm only human you know, nobody's perfect. But, the Lord loves me, that's why He died for me." When I began to understand the extreme sinfulness of sin in my own life, two things happened.

- One: I loathed myself for the fact that I actually enjoyed sin at times. Christ died *for*— Because of—My sins! Thus, I could not make light of the fact—He actually suffered the punishment that I deserved because God the righteous Judge must *punish* sin.
- Two: I had a far deeper appreciation of God's forgiving love through Christ. I can now say—I echo Paul's anguished cry "Wretched man that I am!" I can also say with Him, "While we were yet sinners, CHRIST DIED

FOR US FOR ME!" "The Son of God loved ME and gave Himself for ME!" This realization marks one of the many times I have been

Surprised by Grace!

We must beware of preaching an anemic Gospel, "Jesus loves you, bring your needs to Him, He will meet your needs if you will trust Him." No, it's not wrong to proclaim to the wounded, the broken, the lonely, that Jesus is your answer to these needs. I often use Matthew 11:28-30 to address these issues in peoples lives. Our Lord calls all who are weary with life's burdens, He invites those weighed down with guilt and worry, to come as they are to Him and He promises them rest. He goes on to say, "Take My yoke upon you" that speaks of humble submission, He says, learn of Me . . . this describes the ongoing process of true discipleship. That way you will *find* rest for your soul. Many Christians don't seem to enjoy rest. Instead, they're driven by their need for satisfaction and fulfillment. They expected Christ to meet those needs. Because that does not happen, they either go back to the old ways, or they remain need-centered, undeveloped believers, they have no rest in their soul. They are still in the SELF-ianity stage. Often, this is evidenced by a constant need for counseling. They may be hoping for the counselor to give them a method or a formula whereby their felt needs can be dealt with.

We must notice that in His gracious invitation to find rest, Jesus spoke three key action words, "Come," "Take," "Learn." All three actions are needed in order to find true rest of the soul. To "Come" to Him involves confession that we are sinners to "Take" His yoke requires surrender to Him, and submission to Him, whether our felt needs are met or not. We come to Him with our heavy load, we take intentionally, His yoke of authority upon us, and we begin, and continue, the process of "Learn" from Him. This is how we find rest in our soul.

NOT ERADICATED

After my conversion, to my surprise, and dismay, I discovered that my old sin nature, what the Bible calls the flesh, has not been eradicated. It still sometimes rises up and clamours for attention. Don't we all experience something like this at times? "Why should I put up with this! I'll show him, her, them. . .! Why can't I have my own way for a change?" "Just a little peek at a dirty scene on TV—after all we are under grace, and I'm only human." Right? We feed the flesh. When these temptations arise, that's the time to be ruthless with yourself, to declare "I have been crucified with Christ, my old sin nature belongs in the grave, it has no rights at all anymore." Christians sometimes get involved in arguments that lead to fights, and broken relationships. God's people? How can this be?

In his potent letter the apostle James explains

why. He writes, "What is causing quarrels and fights among you? Isn't it the whole army of evil desires at war within you?" In Galatians 5 we discover that vices which we catagorize as mere human failings, quarrelling, outbursts of anger, jealousy, the feeling that everyone is wrong except you and your little group, these so-called "normal, human" faults, are actually works of the flesh, our old sinful nature. In order to deal with them we go to anger-management seminars, we slot in with programs designed to deal with our addictive behaviour. Be it sexual addiction, alcohol addiction, drug-addiction, and so on. Don't get me wrong. Sometimes these programs can be helpful.

But, here's my point: If we see these problems not as merely human "problems," but as sins, we can then confess, repent of them, surrender them to Christ, and by the power of the Holy Spirit walk in newness of life. While we nurse them as "my problem" it may be that we inadvertently become attached to them, something like Linus's blanket in the Charlie Brown cartoons. We'd actually feel lost without them! I am identified with "my problem" in my thinking! We come across dear Christians who have to have ongoing counseling for "my problem of" anger, lust, jealousy, pornography, and the like. They are looking to Jesus for relief from their problem but they do not see the problem as sin—out and out plain sin, which must be confessed as sin, and repented of. They may well continue struggling along in their SELF-ianity instead of finding true victory by faith in Jesus.

SHIFT YOUR FOCUS

Yes, we are Saved by Grace, God's unmerited favour, through Christ's death on The Cross for our sins. The apostle Paul appeals to the rather wayward Corinthian believers, "I URGE you not to receive the grace of God in vain!" In his opening greeting to them in chapter 1, he addresses them as saints, believers in Christ. In chapter 2 he describes them as carnal by the evidence of their behaviour. Could this be the case with us? If so, we need a shift in focus—from Self, to Saviour, from what He can do for me, to what I must do for Him. Being Christ-centered puts our problems in proper perspective. Because, Jesus is more real to me, I can trust Him fully to deal with my problems. Meanwhile, I go on with Him, serving Him wholeheartedly and finding Him indeed all-sufficient for all my needs.

This shift from SELF-ianity to true CHRIST-ianity is what the Lord requires of each one of us. Paul puts it this way in Romans 8:6, "To be carnally minded [Self-centered] is death, but to be spiritually minded [Christ-centered] is life and peace." Are you ready to make that change? This might help you to do so.

FOUR CASE STUDIES

The Bible describes Christ's work of salvation by using four metaphors for our preconversion state. A slave, a corpse, an enemy and a guilty criminal. Come with me to the old fashioned slave market. Here we have men and women on sale, miserable wretches who are all owned by a ruthless master. They may eat, they may drink, they can move around, but only so far. They are not free—they are under the power of their master, they are compelled to serve him. But, now we see another Person enter the slave market. He pays the price required for their freedom, and He takes them away as His own. Imagine their joy! They are redeemed from their slavery to their former tyrant master! They are now free to serve their new Master who is nothing like the previous one. Serving Him, they discover, is a joy and a privilege! Scripture describes our pre-Christian state as one of slavery.

Our tyrant master is *sin*, we are under its power. We might not all do exceptionally wicked things, but we are nonetheless slaves to sin. You don't agree? Well, don't you ever say, "I know I shouldn't . . . but, I couldn't help myself?" Right! You were under the power of sin, compelled to serve your master, no matter how many New Year's resolutions you may have made! Jesus paid the price to free you from sin, His death on The Cross, in some mysterious way, constituted a transaction that redeemed you, freed you from that bondage. . . "You were not redeemed with . . . silver or gold . . . but with the precious Blood of Christ." (1 Peter 1:18-19 SELECTED) "He gave *himself* for us that He might *redeem* us from all iniquity." (Titus 2:14)

Now, the crucial verse! "You are not your own, for you were bought at a price." (1 Corinthians 6:18-19) Having been redeemed—bought back from sin, we now belong to our new Master Jesus. We have been freed from sin's power, not to "do our own thing," but, to please Him who redeemed us with His *precious* Blood. Christ my Redeemer is the Focus, not me, myself.

The Second Metaphor: Describes our state before conversion is that of a corpse. We are described as "dead in our trespasses and sins." (Ephesians 2:1, 5) You may well be a good athlete, an efficient business person, a professor at a university. No matter what your natural accomplishments may be, if you're not saved, you are disconnected from God, dead, spiritually cut off from Him. Like I was before conversion, you may know about Him but you don't know Him. You're like a keyboard instrument that is not connected to the electricity. Everything about it looks right, but it doesn't do what it was made to do—it doesn't produce musical sounds, because it is not connected to the power outlet, it is dead.

When I surrendered to Jesus and received Him as my own personal Saviour, I actually came alive spiritually! The Bible began to speak to me, it wasn't just a much-revered religious Book. Old hymns my Mom used to play on the piano now moved me, they spoke to me, and when I sang them, the words came from my heart. My likes, my dislikes, my habits began to change, I had come alive in the spirit. It was not a case of turning over a new leaf, I was living a new life, by the power of Christ in me! "God has given us eternal life, and this life is in His Son. He who has the Son of God has the life." (1 John 5:12)

Understanding this transformation from spiritual corpse to resurrected child of God makes me realize how great is my salvation. It's not just a case of becoming religious, and of having my sins forgiven, I have new life, real life, resurrection life in Christ! Thus, I cannot get bogged down in a self-centered form of Christianity. Christ must be central, first, preeminent. Of course, I still experience trials I am subject to temptation. (Jesus had them too!) When I have stumbled, He has always been there to pick me up again. Thus, by faith and the power of the Holy Spirit I can deny the flesh, and "walk in newness of life," daily. (Romans 6:5)

The Third Metaphor: Before conversion I was God's enemy. My mental attitudes, my mind-set, were hostile to the Creator. "You were His enemies, separated from Him by your evil thoughts and actions." (Colossians 1:21 NLT) I wonder if you realize how serious this is! That we mere mortals, can by our mind-set and our behavior be at enmity with

Almighty God! This is how He sees every sinner, there is no neutral ground with Him. This ought to deal with any sentimental ideas we might have about the person who persists in resisting Christ's call to repentance and faith. You ask: but what about God's love for sinners? Have we got it wrong when we tell people that He loves them? No, not at all. Only God, in His perfection, can truly be angry with the resistant sinner, and yet continue to love him and call him to turn and be saved. When we tell of His love in Christ we should also warn of His holy anger should they persist in rejecting him.

BE NOT SENTIMENTAL

We must avoid a sentimental view of The Cross, as if Jesus' death was only a demonstration of how much He loves us, that we should take advantage of His love and commit ourselves to Him in gratitude. Of course, The Cross was the supreme demonstration of His love for sinners. But, what took place on The Cross was a stupendous work of reconciliation between an angry God and His enemies—you and me! Romans 5:10 explains, ". . .While we were *enemies* we were *reconciled* to God by the *death* of His Son!"

You see, when Christ went to The Cross He actually experienced the anger of God that was caused by our rebellion and enmity against Him. A crucial verse in this connection is 1 John 2:2, "He [Jesus] is the *propitiation* for our sins. . ."

The word "propitiation" means "to appease." Imagine, someone who is furious with you raises his hand to strike you. Your friend steps between you and this person, and the blow intended for you falls on your friend. The one who delivered the blow is now appeased, he doesn't want to strike you anymore. That is how God has dealt with the enmity between us and Him. We were destined to receive the blow of God's anger, but, Jesus took it instead. Now God is not angry at us anymore, His anger has been "propitiated" it is appeased and we are now reconciled to Him. This is the case with everyone who truly trusts in Jesus. He and He alone—is the propitiation for our sins. Not our good works, not our good intentions, but Christ, by His death on The Cross. Try to bypass Him and you will come under the blow of God's judgment. Trust in Him, and you can enjoy friendship with God—Now isn't *that*

Surprising Grace!

Do you see why I say we need to understand more fully the Work of the Saviour on The Cross, so we can move away from the SELF-ianity mode, to CHRIST-ianity. Where Jesus is indeed the very Center of our lives? Is He not worthy of that place?

We were slaves to sin, He has *redeemed* us by His Blood. We were *dead* in our sins, cut off from God, and He has given us new life. We were Enemies, and

He has *reconciled* us to God by His death, taking the judgment we should have received. God is thereby *propitiated* and we who believe are brought into Friendship with Him. We must be clear on this, it was not His teachings that have brought all this about, it was His *death* for us on The Cross. "While we were enemies we were reconciled to God by the *death* of His Son." (Romans 5:10) So, if you have trusted in Christ, God is not mad at you! Question: Are you enjoying friendship with Him? If not—WHY not?

The Fourth Metaphor: Before conversion we were *criminals*, on trial before the *Judge*. "How do you plead?" we are asked. "Guilty my Lord" we admit. This is crucial, if we plead "Not Guilty" we are demanding justice. So, tell me, which of us would stand before God the Judge of all the earth, the One who knows all the thoughts of our hearts—and declare we are not guilty of any sin, and that we demand His justice in dealing with us? By pleading guilty we can then ask for *mercy*. That's what you and I need, above everything else, right? Mercy, and forgiveness. Now comes the stupendously surprising action of grace. The Judge has to pass judgment on our crimes, He cannot allow sin to go unpunished in His Universe. His verdict is death. But, instead of you, the guilty sinner, the Judge's own Son steps up and is led away to the execution chamber.

"Christ died for us" remember? In our place, instead of us!

Now what about the guilty criminal, where does

this leave you? The Judge declares you "Not Guilty" you are acquitted because your crimes have been paid for. This has been a simplified explanation of the doctrine of *justification*. As Romans 5:2 has it "We have been justified by faith. . ." Let's look at this word "Justified" and marvel again at God's amazing, surprising grace. Because of Christ's death and my faith in His death for me, God now treats me

Just-as-if—I'd never sinned!

I know I have, you know you have, and of course God the Judge knows. But, here we see the unspeakable value of what Jesus has done in dying for us on The Cross, because He took your place, paid your penalty, the just Judge of all the earth can justly declare you not guilty, and set you (free!). You do not get a suspended sentence, nor are you released because of time served. You are acquitted, set free, justified by faith in Christ. You can shout "Hallelujah" at this point if you so wish! I would be very surprised if you do not so wish!

On a personal note, when I began to understand the doctrine of Justification by faith, that's when I became truly established in my faith. I was able to move from an uncertain up-and-down SELF-ianity to a more settled and robust Christian life. So, let's look at the relevant Scriptures lest you think I've been indulging in theological thumb-sucking!

". . .Being justified freely by His grace through the redemption that is in Christ Jesus." (Romans 3:24-25)

These two verses give us the Source and the Grounds of Justification. The Source is His Grace, not our works. The Grounds on which God can *legally* acquit us sinners. The Redemption that is in Christ, that is—the price He paid. Yet again we see—it was because of The Cross of Jesus, the Blood He shed for us there that we are saved, redeemed, reconciled, and now justified, *not* by His teachings, matchless though they are. How this becomes real to us? "Being justified *by faith* we have peace with God. . ." (Romans 5:2)

OUR FAITH—ANEMIC, OR ROBUST?

Jesus warned of a widespread cooling off of faith and devotion just before His Second Coming. I believe that you and I can ensure against this happening to us, by shifting our focus from SELF to CHRIST, and by becoming established in these doctrines. Of course, we still bring our needs to Him—He is compassionate and merciful. But, I think you'll agree, much of what is taught and preached does not serve to grow us up into Christ— instead it encourages us to remain need-centered. This is how I deal with this tendency in my own life.

I deal with the flesh, my selfishness—ruthlessly. It has no rights—I am crucified with Christ. Of course, I battle often, and I don't always get it right (Ask my Wife!). But, His grace frequently surprises me and "bails me out!" I remember what

He's done for me, I who was once a slave, a corpse, an enemy of God, and a guilty criminal. He has *Freed* this slave, *Quickened* this corpse, *Reconciled* this enemy, and *Justified* this former criminal—this sinner, and declared him "Not Guilty" "Acquitted!" This is

Surprising Grace Indeed!

An ever-growing understanding of the magnitude of His work on The Cross, will help to shift our focus from Self to Christ.

BUT WHAT ABOUT. . .?

I know the question you're wanting to ask. What if we sin after we have been justified by faith? Let me explain: on coming to Faith in Christ we are adopted into God's family. We have been justified, declared not guilty, and the Judge has become our Father! Now we have to learn, as it were, new behaviour. Of course, generally things go well, we are new creations in Christ. But, as I said before, the old nature has not been eradicated—it shows itself from time-to-time, unexpectedly.

In your new family you grab the food before the others, you are disrespectful to your brothers or sisters—that's bad! What does your Father say? "See you again in Court on Monday?" No, not at all. The decision of the court declaring you acquitted was final. You don't go on trial again. Now the father says to you "into the bedroom My child, I have to deal with you"—and He chastens you, as a Father chastens His children whom He loves. Confession of sin and forgiveness follows.

THE BIBLE WORD

What we are talking about here is Sanctification, becoming Holy. Here's how it works. Justification is God's work. "It is God who Justifies." (Romans 8:33) Sanctification is God working in you, and you cooperating. (Philippians 2:12-13) ". . .Work out your salvation . . . for God is at work in you, both to will, and to do His good pleasure."

Justification happens *once*, at your conversion. (Romans 8:29) "Those whom He called He also justified. . ." past tense. It is the *legal* side of salvation. Christ has served your sentence, God the Judge can *legally* acquit you of your sins. Sanctification is a *process* beginning at conversion, and continuing through your life as a Christian. (Hebrews 12:14) "Pursue . . . peace . . . and holiness." (Sanctification) To *pursue* something is not an event, it's a process.

Justification affects your *position*—you're no longer a *criminal* on trial, you are declared not guilty, acquitted! Sanctification relates to your *condition*. You may still be displaying criminal tendencies, at times. Justification is the legal side of your salvation. Christ has served your sentence for your crimes, the Judge can *legally* acquit you on all counts! (Another "Hallelujah!")

Sanctification is the *experiential* aspect—the Holy Spirit working *in* you, purifying you and making you more and more like Jesus, less and less like the old you. In summary—to be Justified: that's what Christ has done *for* you. Being Sanctified—that's what Christ is doing *in* you. Sadly, yes, we do still sin after we are converted. But, as we "work out" the salvation that God by His Spirit is working *in* us, sin becomes the exception, not the general rule. We continue the process of being transformed into the image of His Son, our Saviour.

CHAPTER 12
SIX THINGS PEOPLE NEED, TO GROW

W e Christians are a funny lot! Coming from different backgrounds, different ethnic groups, we each have a story to tell, the story of how the Lord worked in our lives—first to bring us to Himself, and then, to grow us spiritually to where we are right now. Our stories may differ, even as our faces differ—that's the surprising grace of God. But, looking back over 50 years of walking with Him, and over 40-something years as a pastor in His church, I can identify six factors that have been fairly consistent features in the spiritual growth of myself, and of people I have worked with.

The first is ACCEPTANCE

People need to know that God accepts them if they have repented, and that we, God's Community, His church, accept them as well. Romans 15:7 is our guide here. "Therefore, receive one another just as Christ also received us, to the glory of God."

The New Living Translation says, "Accept one another. . ." The Amplified Bible has it: "Welcome one another. . ." In our sin-sick society many people experience rejection. Children are rejected by parents, spouses are rejected by their partners through divorce, faithful employees are rejected by their employers. People are rejected on account of race, the list is endless. These people must know that:

- One: Jesus accepts us just as we are, if we come to Him in humble repentance. "Whoever comes to Me, I will never cast out." (John 6:37[b]) When I surrendered to Christ He didn't say to me, "First change your hairstyle, your clothing, your bad habits, your manner of speaking. Then I'll receive you." He took me as I was—a sinner, miserable, but repentant. The old hymn expresses it so clearly, "Just as I am without one plea, but that Thy Blood was shed for me, that Thou bidst come to Thee, O Lamb of God I come, I come." Every person who under the conviction of the Holy Spirit wants to be saved must know this. We come to Him with all our sins, our shortcomings, our prejudices, and He receives us, He accepts us, He welcomes us and grants us forgiveness.
- Two: We need to do the same to each other. "Welcome one another *as Christ* welcomed us. . ."

NOT MERELY TOLERANCE

Every believer must know that they are not merely tolerated in the community of God, they are Welcomed into it. After all, Jesus taught that the angels in heaven to throw a party over one sinner that repents. We should at least show a genuine interest in one another, and make everyone know that we're glad they are part of God's family.

The second is ASSURANCE

After more than four decades in the ministry I have ceased being surprised to find Christians who still struggle with assurance that they are truly saved, completely forgiven. Some are haunted by an unsavory past, they cannot forget it, so they think the Lord remembers it as well. Some are plagued by their sense of unworthiness. "I have prayed the sinner's prayer, sincerely, but I cannot see how God can forgive me, knowing what I am deep down inside" they reason. This is why I like to share with them the teaching on Justification, set out in the previous chapter. However, some are still plagued be self-condemnation—which is of course the work of the devil.

GUILT—A DOUBLE PROBLEM

This is how the Lord dealt with me when I was struggling as a believer, with a lack of assurance and acceptance. Psychologists speak of Man's two-fold problem when it comes to guilt. The first is Quantitative guilt. It relates to what we have *done*, the sins we've committed.

Qualitative guilt—the guilt of *being*. This relates to what we *are*—our sense of unworthiness, our sinful condition. For me it has been, and continues to be greatly liberating to see that Christ is the answer to this two-fold guilt problem that we all have. The guilt of *doing*—the sins we have committed, Quantitative guilt. Think back to all the wrong things you have done, the lies you have told, or the unkind acts you have perpetrated, think of the worst acts anyone may have done. Now look at Romans 5:6. ". . .Christ died for our sins." That deals with our Quantitative guilt, the guilt for the wrongs we have done.

The guilt of *being*—the sinful nature I struggle with, this dreadful sense that I have of being such an unworthy person, not deserving forgiveness, because of what I am even after being converted. So, let's look at Romans 5 again, this time at verse 8. ". . .While we were sinners, Christ died for *us*." This is not referring to what we have done our sinful acts, although of course, that's included. This is talking about *us*, who we are, unworthy sinners, all of *us*. This is Qualitative guilt.

The good news is—the work Christ accomplished by His death on The Cross dealt with both our sins, and our sinful condition; it dealt with what we have done and with what we are—unworthy of His love and forgiveness. This is *grace*, God giving us what we do not deserve! In Galatians the apostle Paul personalizes it thus: ". . .The Son of God . . . who loved *me* and gave Himself for *me*. . ." This is the man who hunted down Christians and threw them in prison, who described himself as a "wretched man," and confessed, "I know that in me, that is in my flesh dwells *No Good Thing!*" He was fully aware of his unworthiness. He was also convinced that the Lord had received him just as he was, and then by grace made him into the great servant that he became.

RETARDED GROWTH

This sense of uncertainty, this lack of assurance that our guilt has been fully dealt with in Christ, retards and even halts spiritual growth. Point such a person to The Cross, share with them the Scriptures of Paul's testimony. I have found that the Holy Spirit uses this to bring them genuine assurance.

The third is GROWTH

Everyone needs a job to do. We all need to feel we are useful. Someone has said: "You're either a blessing or a blot, you're never a blank!" Every true Christians want is to become a blessing, not a blot. So, the sooner they are put to work, the better it is. Of course, one doesn't give big responsibilities to those new in the faith. We cannot wait until they reach "a certain stage of maturity" giving them some kind of responsibility will actually help them to grow. For example, you can get a new believer to phone people for you about upcoming events, or let them check on attendance figures for your meetings. Let them start there, and see how they shape up. Just as a baby grows by exercise, so a spiritual babe will grow as they begin to serve God in practical ways.

Occasionally, someone says to me, "I want to be used by God but I don't know what my gifts are." I tell them, "Just get busy serving where you can. We need help moving chairs," or "Merle needs help cleaning up after the upcoming Ladies' meal—can you help?" This is a good way to test and see if they, have a servants heart, ready to do menial tasks as needed. I take every opportunity to point them to Galatians 5:13 where Paul writes, ". . .By love serve one another."

I didn't take a course in "finding your gifts" when I got converted. I started off with what I could do—I played the piano for meetings when asked to do so. I was also available to help giving lifts for people, and for moving chairs. As I served in practical ways God opened doors for further ministry.

Merle and I have found that every growing believer is a serving believer. No spectator Christian is a mature Christian! Start them serving as soon as possible! You can ask a new believer, "are you more comfortable working with people, or doing practical service behind the scenes?" Let them make a start there, according to their preference, and watch them progress. Jesus taught that if we're faithful in little things, we will also be faithful with bigger responsibilities. As we grow in service, we grow spiritually.

The fourth is ENCOURAGEMENT

We all need it, from time-to-time! More especially, people still young in the faith. Walking by faith in a God-hostile world sometimes gets us into a spiritual battle. Satan attacks us at our weak points, and we can become despondent, feeling useless or just unappreciated. Then the danger is, we can give way to self-pity, we become "poor-me" centered, or our hearts may become hardened, and our growth in Christ retarded. This is why the writer to the Hebrews writes: ". . .Encourage one another daily . . . lest any of you become hardened by the deceitfulness of sin." (Hebrews 3:13)

I've noticed a strange phenomenon in some believers when they become discouraged and who are having a "dry spell" spiritually. They stay away from church meetings. Then they complain that God seems disinterested in their plight! That's something like a man who is dehydrated, and instead of coming to the water fountain, he stays away. You ask him, "why don't you come to the fountain and drink?" He answers: "because I feel dehydrated!"

Surely, that's the time for him to get to the fountain and have some water to cure his problem!

It's at the gathering of God's blood-bought people that we can encourage one another, and where the Holy Spirit moves upon us, revealing Christ to our hearts and refreshing us as we worship the Lord together. Thus, the writer to the Hebrews instructs us: "Let us not neglect our meeting together, as some people do, but *encourage* and warn each other, especially now that the day of His coming back again is drawing near." (Hebrews 10:25 NLT)

We must encourage believers to *be* at the meetings regularly, and we must encourage each other at every opportunity to keep faithful in our attendance. These "come-togethers" are like the water fountain in my illustration—where we drink of the Spirit of God and come away refreshed and revitalized.

ME TOO!

Over the years, I have often been the recipient of much-valued encouragement. People send brief messages on Thank You cards, or I receive a phone call from someone expressing appreciation for our labours. These have sometimes come just at a low moment in my life, and have served to lift my spirits again. A *stand-out* example happened some years back, and I shall always remember it with gratitude. I shared with a colleague who lived several hundred miles away, that I was really struggling with a certain issue in my ministry. This dear man, unasked, hopped aboard a plane, came and spent the day with me, then flew back home that night. He didn't come to counsel me, he just came to listen, to talk, to pray with me for God's direction. I felt so encouraged, and of course extremely grateful to the Lord for such a practical demonstration of true Christian fellowship—that is: sharing together, burdens as well as blessings. The problem in question didn't go away, but, I was better equipped to deal with it through the encouragement of this brother, and in time, God worked it all out for good. This reminds me of the account of Jonathan and David which features in 1 Samuel 23:16.

STRENGTHENED IN GOD

David, you will remember, had been anointed King in Saul's place. But, Saul was still in power, and was hunting for David to kill him. Think how young David must have felt at this time. Some of the Psalms expressing his distress were written during this period when he was hiding in the wilderness from Saul's soldiers.

In 1st Samuel 23 verse 16 we read: "Then Jonathan, Saul's son arose and went to David in the woods and strengthened his hand in God." The New American Standard Bible (NASB) puts it this way, "he encouraged him in God." I like that, don't you! We must note, encouragement is not flattery, nor does it amount to merely propping up a person psychologically. We encourage people so that they can draw strength from the Lord for themselves, and continue to carry out their responsibilities for Him in the power of His Spirit. David still had a long spell to endure as a fugitive from Saul. But, having been encouraged, he grew strong and finally took his rightful place on the throne of Israel.

GROWING PEOPLE FOR GOD

To grow into Christlike maturity, we all need Acceptance from God and one another, we need Assurance, that the Lord has indeed dealt with our *sins*, what we have done, as well as our *sin*—what we are, unworthy, but, completely forgiven in Christ. We need a job to do, so that we can Grow in service and in responsibility, we need Encouragement to lift our spirits when the going gets tough, so that we can *keep* going.

The fifth is CORRECTION

I don't think anyone really enjoys being told: "What you did/said was wrong. You need to correct that." None of us can ever get to the place in our Christian walk where we don't need to be corrected at some point or other. It's essential to our growth in Christ. We'll only be perfect when we get to heaven. The writer of Proverbs is very blunt. He states: "He who hates correction is stupid." (Proverbs 12:1) Indeed, to reject godly rebuke or correction is to reject an opportunity to grow and to develop as a fruitful follower of Christ. A stern, rebuke motivated by a genuine concern for the person may protect them from serious mistakes, if it is received with the right attitude. The Lord Jesus frequently corrected His 12 disciples. Sometimes, it was a mild rebuke, occasionally it was quite severe.

When they returned from a successful mission, celebrating the fact that the demons that afflicted people were subject to them in His Name, He told them to rather rejoice in that their names were written in heaven. (Luke 10:20) When they began to panic when a storm on the sea threatened to capsize their boat, Jesus rebuked the storm and it subsided. Then He rebuked them: "Why are you so fearful? How is it that you have no faith?" (Mark 4:39-40)

When some of His disciples came requesting special positions of authority in His coming kingdom, He rebuked their worldly ambition for privilege and power and instructed them to embrace a servant attitude instead, just as He did. (Mark 10:42-45)

He reserved the most severe rebuke for Peter. This zealous apostle, you may remember, actually began to rebuke the Lord for talking about going to Jerusalem where He would be tortured and crucified. Perhaps, if our Lord had taken a course on public relations, He would have said something like this to Peter. "My dear friend, I'm sure you mean well. But, you need to understand. . ." That's not what happened! (Just kidding of course!) "Get behind me Satan!" the Lord said. "You are an offense to Me, for you are not mindful of the things of God, but the things of men." Let me ask—how would you have reacted, had the Lord said this to you? Remember, this was in the hearing of the other disciples! I suspect many of us may have reacted something like this: "There's no love in this church!" "I resent being spoken to like that. . ." "Well! I'm obviously not appreciated here! I think I must leave!"

Peter took the rebuke, kept following His Master, and became a leading apostle in the Early Church. You see, Peter with all his faults, had a humble, teachable spirit, so he continued to grow. That goes for you and me too. If we keep humble, if we remain teachable, the Lord will see to it that we keep on growing up into Christ. ". . .He chastens us for our profit, that we might be sharers of His holiness!" Think of THAT! (Hebrews 12:10 ACCEPTED)

A word on *How* to profit from rebuke or correction. Job 5:17 states: "Behold, happy is the man whom the Lord corrects." But, the Lord often uses people to correct us, and sometimes, people whom we might not really like! Whether the person correcting you is doing so gently, or not-so-gently, do these three things. *Hear* it, *Sift* it to see how it applies to you, and then *Act* on it. That way, you will continue to grow to Christlike maturity. It's vital that we teach believers—especially new converts—the value of godly correction. It is essential to our growth in Christ.

The sixth is AFFIRMATION

This goes together with my previous point, that of correction. When you have rebuked someone, particularly if the rebuke has been rather severe, it's very important that you follow up within a day or so, with a word of affirmation. Example: In his first Letter to the Corinthians, Paul instructs them to put a willfully sinful man out of the fellowship. In his second letter written a while later, he has obviously heard of this man's repentance. So, in chapter 2 he urges them to forgive the transgressor and comfort him, lest he be swallowed up with too much sorrow. "Therefore, I urge you to affirm your love to him" he writes in verse 8.

Admittedly, this is an extreme case. We need to do this with almost any case where we have had to rebuke someone, *provided that* they have received the correction with humility.

One occasion stands out for me in this regard. Together with a colleague in leadership, I had to speak strongly to someone about the way he had delivered a certain message. Apart from the fact that several people were hurt and confused, his remarks were simply not in line with our Biblical views on a particular issue. Again, we were prayerful, looking to God for wisdom and sensitivity. How can you tell a man "you were at fault in what you said," without telling him straight out that he was wrong? It was a difficult encounter and the brother was obviously stung by the rebuke, but, he took it quietly. A couple of days later I sent him an email telling him "thanks for hearing us" and expressing our appreciation for his devotion to the Lord and to the church. I'm glad to report, our relationship suffered no harm as a result, and the brother has continued his very promising ministry.

People need to be guided as they minister for the Lord, whatever area that ministry might be. They need to have regular feedback, "You're doing well" and when necessary, they need to have their errors pointed out. Don't do it that way, do it this way." Generally, speaking they will welcome the correction, and go on growing. Should they refuse the correction, that too must be addressed, to make them realize — we all have to be open to correction, that's part of our growing up into Christ. You may have to address a rebellious attitude — a more serious fault in any believer. I often point out the Scripture that equates rebellion with the sin of witchcraft. When one has delivered a sharp rebuke, follow it up with a word of appreciation for the person concerned. Affirming the brother or sister can work wonders, they feel encouraged, valued, and they continue to grow in Christ.

ANY MORE POINTS?

Of course, there are other factors involved in our spiritual growth and progress. Believers must be regularly reading and studying the Bible. They must be encouraged to seek to be filled with the Holy Spirit. These six factors constitute the "human responsibility" side of every believer's spiritual development into a mature, Christlike disciple.

CHAPTER 13
UN-Dead CHRISTIANS

———— ❧⦁❧ ————

"Come to Jesus, He will forgive you and give you new life." That's our message to the not-yet believer. Yeah, Yeah! The divorce rate among Christian couples matches closely that of non-Christians! This, in spite of the Bible teaching that God hates divorce!

How does one account for this? Why is it that, in personal conflict situations at work for example, Christians, instead of being part of the solution ("Blessed are the Peacemakers") are often part of the problem? Here's one more! Why is it that some believers, gifted by the Lord, go on well for a while, serving usefully in the church in some capacity, then leave in a huff because someone has offended, criticized or misunderstood them? ("Blessed are the Meek—the Merciful.") The Beatitudes quoted in parenthesis show that such behaviour is in direct opposition to what Jesus requires in His followers.

TWINKLE, OR SHINE?

You may be thinking: "Well that's just human nature! We're not perfect, right?" Right! Still, we are described as "the light of the world." Our Lord did not say "Let your light *twinkle* in a moderate measure—just as long as you're just a little better than the nonbeliever." He said: "Let your light *shine* in such a way that people will *see*. . ." Surely that means that our behaviour should be different, and that we should thereby attract others to Him! As I see it, the problem is, we are "UN-Dead Christians." Let me explain: Sure, our message to the world is "come to Jesus, be saved from your sins, receive new life."

The New Testament abounds with instructions to believers to realize and apply the truth that—believing in Christ means death to ourselves, realizing that in God's economy we have been crucified with Christ. He died for us, so we are dead—to ourselves, to our old sinful nature. The catch is—we have to work it out, we have to apply that "co-death" with Christ in order to truly experience our "co-resurrection" with Him to a new life. The Lord gives us many opportunities in daily life, to demonstrate that we are truly "crucified with Christ!" For example: In marriage, our selfish, please-me-first attitudes are frequently challenged. In some situations we have to *choose* to please our spouse, rather than to have our own way. In interpersonal conflicts at work, and in our church life we often have opportunities to show that we are dead to our selfish nature and alive to God, by the way we react—or *don't* react—to a given situation.

Let me share with you something of my struggles in this area. I must warn you, lest you be disappointed—there'll be no confession of gory secrets! Sorry! Only the basic principles! Early on in my walk with the Lord I was made to realize, through preachers and through books I was reading, that I was to die to self, in order to be alive to God. A verse that particularly challenged me was where Jesus said: "Except you *deny* yourself, take up The Cross and follow Me, you cannot be My disciple." I was serious about my faith, so I determined to deny myself. I thought that, once the decision was made, self was out of the picture, dead. I could now follow Jesus fully. The only trouble I expected to encounter was being persecuted by the unconverted.

Can you imagine my consternation at realizing—Self was not dead, but very much alive, and I was at times *very* susceptible to all the old temptations of passionate desires, and of the Ego! This, in spite of my fervent, determined renunciation of the monster! For a while, I wondered again if I was really saved! Yet again, God in His surprising grace taught me. I learned that, to deny self simply means: I give my old nature no place, he has no rights. Crucified with Christ, my "old man" the old me, belongs in the grave.

When he tries, rise up—and I experience many attempted "resurrections" of the old nature, I deny him his right to express himself. I give him no leeway. That's how it ought to work! Let me set it out this way. Truth is Objective. It's like the Law of Gravity—it works whether you believe it and experience it, or not. If you doubt this, climb on the roof and then step off. You'll be an instant believer in the Law of Gravity, but alas—too late! You will experience—the objective, unaltereable truth of the Law of Gravity! (Please do *not* climb on the roof—I'm only kidding—it's just an illustration!)

Faith, real faith is Subjective. I put my trust in God's objective truth—say—His promise of forgiveness, and now I *know* I'm forgiven. I experience that truth for myself—it's not "out there," it's real to me. The *objective* truth has become *subjective*—I don't merely acknowledge it, I experience it.

Just so: God's Word tells us that, as believers, we have been *crucified with Christ*. It's the Objective truth of what happened at The Cross. Now, I am instructed in Romans, "Know that your old nature has been crucified with Christ. . ." "Consider yourself *dead* unto sin. . ." "walk in NEWness of life!" This is the *subjective* outworking of that truth. It is working in my life.

Let's take another look. We can talk about Position, and Condition. On conversion, through faith in Jesus, my *position* is: I died with Christ. This is the Objective truth, it's what the Bible says.

The way I *live* my life daily should show that I am truly *dead* to my old sinful nature, that I am now living a *new* life. This is my *condition*. Truth is now subjective, I live it out.

The apostle Paul put it like this: "I am crucified with Christ. Nevertheless, I live, yet not I, but Christ lives in me, and the life I *now* live [note, a changed life!] . . . the life *I now* live, I live by faith in the Son of God who loved me and gave Himself for me."

You may be wondering: does this destroy my individuality? Is my personality crucified? Fair question! Answer: of course not! For me, Galatians 5:24 best explains it. It says: "Those who are Christ's have crucified the flesh with its passions and lusts." (NKJ) The NLT says this: "Those who belong to Christ have nailed the passions and desires of their sinful nature to His Cross and crucified them there." See, it's not your personality that is crucified, it's your sinful desires, your "me-first" mind set that is crucified. If before conversion you had a quick wit, you will still have a quick wit, but it will be sanctified, it won't be hurtful to anyone, and it certainly won't be coarse or vulgar. If you had an analytical mind, always attending to details, you will still be the same, only that faculty will be sanctified, fit for the Master's use. Let's look at the apostle Paul as an example.

Before he was converted, Paul was a great scholar, a very learned man, a person of great determination. We see this in the way he went about ruthlessly persecuting Christ's followers, intent on stamping out this movement. Once converted, he displayed the same unrelenting determination to spread the Gospel to all the world. His great intellect, now sanctified, is displayed in his writings, especially in that "Everest of Epistles," the Letter to the Romans.

To be crucified with Christ does not eradicate who you are. It subdues, yes, nullifies the power of your old sinful desires, your ungodly habit patterns. You have new motivations, a new focus away from Self. You are more God-focused and "Other-centered." I believe two marriage partners who daily seek to apply this truth, will always be able to work out their relational problems with God's help. Failing to do so tells me that one at least, is an UN-Dead Christian, the old selfish "please me first" nature is resurrected. Result? Unresolved conflicts at work, childish tantrums that cause people to leave the church, and sadly, Christian marrieds getting divorced.

But, you say — the resurrections I experience of the Old Man are sometimes so powerful, I am often defeated. My bad temper, my jealousies, my lusts, these are often too strong for me and I fall again into sin. Same here! But, let's get God's remedy for these unwanted resurrections. (Romans 8:13) "For if you live according to the flesh you will die. But, if by the Spirit you put to death the deeds of the flesh you will live."

I see two vital truths here. The first: we must not pamper the flesh. Away with the cop out phrase, excusing our fleshly lapses, "Oh well, nobody's perfect!" A tolerant attitude to the flesh brings spiritual death. "If you live according to the flesh you will die!" The second: The Holy Spirit aids us in this conflict. We render the old man ineffective by the power of the Holy Spirit working in us. This is why the command: "Be filled [continuously] with the Spirit" is so important to obey. It is by His power that we can overcome these unwelcome resurrections of our old nature.

I can't fight my old nature successfully just through my determination. Envy, jealousy, lust and uncontrolled anger or rage, these manifestations of the flesh can often break out even though I'm vigilant, and ruthless with the old nature. I have to invoke the Holy Spirit to aid me. I seek to be filled again and again. That's the only way I can avoid behaving like an UN-Dead Christian! Here's a great promise in this regard: "Walk in the Spirit and you will *not* fulfill the lust of the flesh." (Galatians 5:16)

As we learn to conduct our lives daily under the influence of the Holy Spirit, the fruit of the Spirit, that is, the character traits of Christ become more evident. Now here's another confession—confidentially of course! I used to read the description of the fruit of the Spirit in Galatians 5, you know—love, joy, peace, self control, patience, etc. and become very discouraged. The reason? I recognized that, while I showed some of these traits in a measure, I knew I was falling far short of what the Lord required. I fluctuated between determination (*I will* show more love, self control, etc.) and despair. (I'm a poor example of a Christian!) Have you been there?

Finally, the penny dropped! The *fruit* of the Spirit, of course! Fruit must be cultivated, it takes *time* to grow. It's not the result of Christian determination, of trying harder. Fruit! Fruit *grows* when cultivated and nurtured. Romans 6:13 was a help here "Yield yourself to God." Yielding does not involve effort, it speaks of surrender. Today, after five decades as a Christ follower, I still have to yield to the Lord daily. If I don't, the old nature pops up again. As I yield my self-will to the Lord, the character traits of Jesus become evident, not by my efforts but, by the Spirit of God working in me, and the blessed process is ongoing.

TO SUM UP!

We must avoid settling for a self-centered form of Christianity. We don't want to be seen as UN-Dead Christians. Our Saviour must not merely be *prominent* in our lives, He must be PRE-eminent. We must recognize that our flesh, our old nature, is at enmity with God. Thus, we must not pamper the flesh, we must be ruthless, and *deny* it any rights. We Christ followers are "Crucified with Christ," the old nature has no place in our lives. If we suffer a "relapse" into our old ways—rage, lust, envy, or whatever—run *to* the Lord, don't run from Him! Confess the sin, renounce it, and thank Him that His Blood continues to cleanse us from *all* sin. (1 John 1:7, 9) We must seek the in filling of the Holy Spirit daily, for it is only by His power that we overcome the flesh.

Remember, for fruit to grow it needs to be nurtured and cultivated. Read the Bible, meditate on the Word, be consistent in your attendance at the church meetings. Don't be a spectator, be active for the Lord, and endeavour to *apply* what God says to you, daily, and the fruit of the Spirit will become more and more evident. "Since we have been united with Him in His death, we will also be raised as He was. Our old sinful selves were crucified with Christ so that sin might lose its power in our lives." (Romans 6:5-6 NLT) "I have come that they might have *life*, more abundantly." (John 10:10)

CHAPTER 14
BAPTISM IN THE SPIRIT, TONGUES, AND SUCH LIKE

The first time I heard someone speaking in tongues was when I attended a Sunday morning baptismal service in the Assembly of God in East London, South Africa. It scared me nearly to kingdom come! I was not yet converted, and stranger to the Pentecostal style of service. What was I doing there? Answer: a cute young "chick" who was boarding with my brother Joe and his wife Stella had invited me to witness her baptism. She was cute! (Did I mention that? It's worth repeating!) Her name was Merle. It was an invitation I could not refuse!

During the service I was startled to hear people speak out loudly and passionately in a foreign language. I was so startled, I nearly jumped out of my skin! After each utterance someone else spoke in English, with equal passion. I found out later that this was the Biblically required interpretation of the unknown tongue. Once I was truly converted I was encouraged to seek the Lord for the Baptism in the

Holy Spirit. The teaching was clear the Baptism was for every believer and it would enable me to speak in tongues, like so many were doing in our fellowship. I wasn't excited about the prospect. To be honest, I was of the opinion that people who spoke in tongues were, well, a little strange! I didn't want to be like them! I loved the Lord, I was learning the Word, and I was serving Him with my musical ability. Wasn't that enough?

I remember saying to one of the singers in my music group "I am going on with the Lord, but I wish He was more real to me." Her reply, "That will happen when you're baptized with the Spirit." This spurred me on to attend "receiving meetings" where seekers would be prayed for to receive the baptism. However, each of these meetings left me unfilled, and greatly discouraged. As I was praying, I was disturbed that those around me were getting filled and babbling off loudly in tongues, but nothing was happening to me.

You've probably heard this caricature of the prayer helpers in some such cases—one encourages you—"Hold on brother." The next exhorts, "Let go brother," while yet another urges, "Reach out brother!" Well, my experience wasn't quite so comical, but it came close! Result, I went away greatly discouraged. I felt left out—unloved. I couldn't speak in tongues!

Yet again, God surprised me with His grace. Over a few months He graciously brought me to a place where I had a real hunger and thirst for Him, not just for tongues. A passage of Scripture that really helped me was John 7:37-39(a). "If any man *thirst* let Him come to Me and drink. . ." I began to realize I had been primarily seeking to speak in tongues, rather than seeking to be filled with the Holy Spirit, God Himself.

I invited one of our elders to come to our home and pray with me and Merle one evening. There, it happened! I was flooded with joy as I drank of the spiritual water that Jesus offered, and I found myself laughing, sputtering out strange words, and—hold you breath—rolling across the carpet in our living room! My poor sister Micky who was also present, was, I think, put off by this less than respectable reaction, while Merle, pregnant with Delray, was quietly speaking in her new prayer language.

No, I was not transformed into a spiritual giant by the baptism in the Spirit. But, there were several effects evidenced in my life from then on.

- Jesus became more real to me—as my singer friend had promised.
- I was more acutely aware of the sinfulness of sin, and studiously tried to avoid it.
- I was experiencing in a deeper dimension of God's love for me.
- Passages of Scripture became more alive to me. They spoke into my life in a relevant way.
- Shy as I was of public speaking, I now had a boldness I never knew previously.

I must emphasize—the Spirit's baptism does not make us perfect, or mature. He comes primarily to empower us to *be* witnesses for the Saviour. (Acts 1:8) "You will receive power [ability-energy] after the Spirit comes upon you and you shall *be* My witnesses. . ." I must state also baptism in the Spirit is not a goal to be attained, then to sit back. After the initial in filling of the Holy Spirit, one needs to be filled repeatedly, to live a fruitful and victorious Christian life. This is the context of Ephesians 5:18 where we are commanded ". . .Be filled [continuously] with the Holy Spirit."

OBJECTIONS

Many Christians—fine, dedicated believers do not accept that the Baptism is a separate experience from conversion. They maintain that the apostles prayed for the new converts in Jerusalem and Samaria and Ephesus to be filled at the inauguration—if you like—of the New Covenant. That's when the Spirit was newly given, they say. Since then, there is no need, we get it all at conversion. There is no need for a separate "Baptism in the Spirit."

MORE THAN ONE

The fact is: there are at least three separate baptisms mentioned in the New Testament. You ask: "how can I know which is which?" Simple:

Ask these three questions each time a baptism is mentioned.
- Who is the Baptizer?
- Who is the Candidate?
- Who or what is the Element into which the candidate is to be baptized?

THE FIRST BAPTISM

"By one Spirit are we all baptized into one Body." (1 Corinthians 12:13) Note: The Baptizer is the Holy Spirit. The Candidate "We" new believers. The Element—the Body—the Church of Jesus Christ. This is *conversion*, when we are born again and are spiritually joined together or immersed into Christ's Body, the church.

THE SECOND BAPTISM

Baptism in water, a command in the New Testament for all who are converted to Christ. (Acts 2:38) "Repent and be baptized, every one of you. . ." Here the Baptizer is a church leader. The Candidate, the converted sinner, the Element, water.

THE THIRD BAPTISM

The Baptism with the Holy Spirit. ". . .He [Jesus] will baptize you with the Holy Spirit and fire." (Matthew 3:11) In John chapter 1, John the Baptist sees the Spirit descending like a dove upon Jesus. He writes, ". . .He who sent me to baptize with water said to me, upon whom you see the Spirit descending and remaining on Him—this is *He who baptizes with the holy spirit.*" Here, the Baptizer is Jesus. The Candidate is the Believer, and the Element is the Holy Spirit.

We must not confuse this baptism with the baptism in 1 Corinthians 12. There, the Baptizer is the Holy Spirit—that's conversion. Here the Baptizer is Jesus, this is for power to be a witness. (Acts 1:8)

Let's look at it this way, *The Father's Gift to a Lost World is His Son.* "For God *so* loved the world that He gave His only Son, that whoever believed in Him would not perish. . ." (John 3:16) "Whosoever" that means anyone may receive Him as Saviour if they repent. The Spirit then baptizes, or immerses them into the mystical Body of Christ, His church. Then, *The Son's Gift to his church is the Holy Spirit.*

". . .If I depart I will send Him to you. . ." (John 16:7) ". . .Exalted to the right Hand of God He [Jesus] has received from the Father the promised Holy Spirit and has poured out what you now see and hear." (Acts 2:33)

TO CLARIFY

The not-yet-converted *cannot* receive the Holy Spirit. Only those who are saved can receive Him. Jesus said: "The world cannot receive Him because it neither sees Him nor knows Him." (John 14:17) If you've been saved you have the Holy Spirit. He has been working in you, bringing you to Christ. He has brought about the born-again experience—the new birth in you. Now you need to be filled with the Spirit. Here's another way of putting it. The Spirit whom we did not know, convicted us and brought us to Jesus, causing us to be born again. Now Jesus says: "I want to introduce you to the One who brought you to Me," and He immerses us in the Spirit.

KEY QUESTIONS

Since coming to faith in Christ, have you experienced the baptism in the Spirit? If not, why not? "The promise is to you, to your children, to as many as the Lord God shall call." (Acts 2:39)

If you have been baptized with the Spirit, are you being filled regularly? The apostles in Acts 2 were filled on the Day of Pentecost. A while later Acts 4 records, "and they were all filled with the Holy Spirit." (Again!) This ongoing, repeated in filling of the Spirit is what is referred to in Ephesians 5:18. "Don't get drunk with wine but be filled with the Spirit."

WOULD YOU LIKE TO BE FILLED?

"Yes," you say, but you ask, "How?" Here are two simple pointers that helped me. Simple, child-like faith. Remember, receiving the Spirit is a *gift*, not a reward. Jesus said: "Everyone who asks, receives." (Luke 11:10) Come to the Lord expecting Him to fulfill His promise, and fill you.

STRONG SPIRITUAL THIRST

"If you are *thirsty*, come to Me and drink." (John 7:37-39[a]) For the Scriptures declared that rivers of living water will flow out from within (the person who so drinks). Jesus fills you as you drink, and then the Spirit flows out from your life as you serve Him in love.

HOW WILL YOU KNOW THAT YOU HAVE RECEIVED THE HOLY SPIRIT?

As was the case with me, Christ will become more real to you. Jesus said: "He will glorify Me." (John 16:14) The Scriptures will be become alive and more understandable to you. "He . . . the Spirit of Truth, will guide you into all Truth." (John 16:13) You will experience the love of God, *for you*, and *through you*, in a new measure. (Romans 5:5) "The love of God is poured into our hearts by the Holy Spirit."

You will have greater boldness to speak out for Christ. (Acts 1:8) "You will receive power after the Holy Spirit has come upon you, and you will be My witnesses. . ." (Acts 4:31) "When they had prayed—they were all filled with the Holy Spirit and *spoke* the Word of God with *boldness*." These are some of the signs you will experience. But, the initial sign recorded in the Book of Acts, which records how it all began—is: "They spoke with other tongues."

Of the five occasions recorded in the Book of Acts of people receiving the Spirit *initially*, three times it states: "They spoke in tongues." (Acts 1:4; 10:44; 19:6) For the other two occasions, no mention is made of any sign, just the statement that they received the Gift of the Holy Spirit. (Acts 8:17) The Samaritan converts, and Acts 9:17, Saul, who later was called Paul the great apostle. We must note however, that Paul later wrote to the Corinthian church "I thank my God that I speak with tongues more than you all!"

We must note also, when the Samaritans received, (Acts 8) Simon the sorcerer saw something happen to these people that caused him to want to buy the ability to pray for people to get baptized with the Spirit! So, what do you think he saw, that made him want to buy the gift? The Bible doesn't say. I leave it to you to draw your own conclusions based on the evidence that you have of the other recorded instances.

A WORD OF CAUTION

If you are seeking the Baptism in the Spirit, *Don't* make the mistake I made! Don't seek to speak in tongues, seek to be filled with the Holy Spirit! I only got the Baptism when I sought the Lord, I spoke in tongues as a consequence of receiving the

Holy Spirit.

On occasion I have prayed for people to receive and they have come under a heavy anointing of the Spirit. But, they only spoke in tongues some hours after, and in some cases—some days after prayer. Thirst for the Spirit, ask for the Spirit, don't get sidetracked on tongues. When you're filled, that will come.

BENEFITS OF PRAYING IN TONGUES

In 1 Corintians 14 the apostle Paul thanks God that he speaks in tongues, and lists some of the benefits of praying in tongues (praying with the Spirit, as it is sometimes called).

- We speak mysteries in the Spirit. (vs 2)
- We build ourselves up spiritually. (vs 4)
- We can praise God in tongues and give Him thanks. (vs 6)

DOESN'T PAUL MINIMIZE THE IMPORTANCE OF TONGUES?

No, far from downplaying the importance of tongues-speaking, the apostle writes, "I wish you *all* spoke in tongues." (1 Corinthians 14:5) In the church meeting, he urges that we would seek to prophesy. You see, when I pray in tongues, I and I alone am edified. That's fine, I need to be built up. In the meeting we want the congregation to be edified, so prophecy is more to be desired. Let me explain: Tongues is inspired speech in a language not understood by neither speaker nor hearers. Prophecy is inspired speech in the vernacular (in our case, in English). Therefore, it brings blessing to all who hear it. Tongues in a public meeting must be interpreted so all can benefit from the utterance. Thus the apostle writes, "Let the one who speaks in tongues [in the public meeting] pray that he/she may interpret [another gift of the Spirit] that all may be edified."

I've taken the time to elaborate on speaking in tongues because there seems to be a lot of misunderstanding about the subject. Let me conclude this chapter by explaining the benefits I derive from praying in tongues. There are times when my mind is dull, I don't know what to say to God apart from "Praise the Lord, Thank you Jesus, Hallelujah." Then I lift my heart and my voice to Him in the prayer language the Spirit has given me, and in a short time I am strengthened and refreshed in my spirit, able to pray intelligently once more. I don't know what I said in a tongue, but the Lord knows. No, it's not gibberish "In the spirit we speak mysteries," Paul writes. (1 Corinthians 14:2) We can be praising God, giving thanks to Him. (1 Corinthians 14:16) We can be interceding for a great need. (Romans 8:26)

This seems to have been the case in the following story I am about to relate.

SLEEP—DRIVING

Some years ago a colleague of mine got out of bed in the middle of the night, got into his car and began to drive down the main street of his town, *on the wrong side of the road.* Another vehicle filled with late-night revelers came straight at him, and a head-on collision seemed inevitable. But, at the last moment Brian woke up (he had been driving in his sleep) and turned his vehicle out of the path of the oncoming car. The next afternoon he spoke at a meeting some miles away on a church member's farm. After relating the story of his miraculous escape, one of the woman said, "Now I know why the Lord woke me up last night!" She related how she had awoken with a deep concern for Brian, but did not know how to pray, as she did not know the particular need . . . So, she just prayed fervently in tongues for some time, until the burden lifted, whereupon she went back to bed and slept peacefully. Checking the respective times with her and Brian, it was found to be at about the time of his nocturnal escapade that she began to pray in the Spirit for him. Coincidence? I don't think so! A dedicated disciple of Christ was obedient to the promptings of the Holy Spirit, prayed in her prayer language for her minister, and the Lord intervened and saved him from a terrible accident!

DOES THIS BAPTISM MAKE ME A SUPER-CHRISTIAN?

No, it does not. The baptism in the Spirit gives me power to be a witness, it makes Jesus more real to me. I have to *walk* by the Spirit. I have to *apply* The Cross in my daily life, denying my fleshly desires and *yielding* to Him as He works in me to make me more like Jesus. The Baptism gives the power, I still have to make the choice to yield to His working. I still have to exercise *faith*, to see Him work in my life that which pleases Him.

The late Corrie ten Boom, Holocaust survivor who became a world-traveled Bible teacher, said this referring to Ephesians 5:18. The most joyous command in the Bible is: "Be filled with the Spirit!"

She's right!

CHAPTER 15
ASPIRATION, CONCERNS, DELIGHTS

I want to finish this book by sharing with you three things that tend to occupy my mind quite prominently. Remember my story at the beginning of chapter 1? I told of the old man who, when asked, "Have you lived here all your life?" replied, "Not yet!" While I'm still here, in the "not yet" stage, I cherish some specifics.

ASPIRATIONS

I'm not ready to sit down in the departure lounge of Celestial Airways, just waiting for the call to get on board for final destination Heaven, imminent though the call might be. I want to be like Caleb, who, at 85 years of age, said: "Now give me this mountain" and even though he had to fight the giants to get it, he got it! Whether my call out of "here" comes sooner, or later, I want the Lord to work in me to make me:

- A better teacher of the Word.

Before every message, I always pray that the Word which I bring will be more than just interesting Bible information. I pray that the Holy Spirit will impact hearts and lives, that we, preacher and hearers alike, will *apply* what we hear from God's Word. I don't want to be a one-theme preacher. I want to be able to say as Paul said to the Ephesians elders, "I have not shunned to declare to you the whole counsel of God." I aspire to be a more effective preacher and teacher of the Word. I want to preach and teach the Word in places where they don't have much in the way of Bible resources. Here in the States, we have some fine preachers. There's no shortage of videos, DVDs, and audio material if people want it. I love to minister here, don't get me wrong! But, I have a greater joy in ministering the unsearchable riches of Christ, in places like Malawi, India and the like, where they don't have much access to the printed or recorded Word. That is why I visit each of those two countries every year. My goal is well described in Colossians 1:28. "We proclaim Him [Christ] warning every man and teaching every man, that we may present every man *mature* in Christ."

• I aspire to be a better husband.

The Lord has blessed me with a truly excellent woman for a wife, and the longer we are together the more I appreciate her outstanding qualities. It's also true that, as I look back on our half century of married life, I realize that I have often been insensitive and inconsiderate to her, especially in the earlier years when I was preoccupied with trying to establish myself as a capable minister of the Gospel. Although, we never had serious problems in our relationship, I came close at times to duplicating the error referred to in Song of Solomon, "They made me a keeper of their vineyards, but my own vineyard I have not kept." Sure, I could be patient and understanding in ministering to members of the congregation, but when I came home, this "Man of God, the Man of faith and power" could be irritable, short with Merle and the children, and in general, quite crabby and insensitive! The church vineyard was well cared for, but, if it wasn't for Merle, our family vineyard would at times have been overgrown with the weeds of selfishness and inattention. I'm a lot better now, I think! (Please, Lord!) I continue to aspire to be a better, more Christlike husband.

Above all, I aspire to be. . .

   less like me and

      progressively more and more like Jesus.

SO MUCH AND TOO MUCH

It's wonderfully true that God loves us *so much*, He accepts us just as we are, and forgives all our sins through what His Son did for us on The Cross. It's equally true that God loves us *too much* to leave us just as we are. His purpose for you and me is this: that we should be conformed to the image of His Son, the Lord Jesus Christ. (Romans 8:29)

Now let's not get all mystical about this! To be

like Jesus doesn't mean we have an ethereal appearance, and float a few feet off the ground, that we only say deeply spiritual things to people, or that we become soft and effeminate powder-puff people! On the contrary, to be like Jesus is to be truly *manly*!

CHRISTLIKE? WHAT DOES THAT LOOK LIKE?

We have a detailed description of what a Christlike character really is, in Galatians 5. There we have listed the fruit of the Spirit, which really amounts a nine-fold description of our Lord: love, joy, peace, longsuffering, kindness, goodness, faithfulness, gentleness, self-control. We see all these attributes displayed in the account of His life in the four Gospels, Matthew, Mark, Luke and John. This is what the Holy Spirit wants to produce in your life and mine. Without being falsely modest, I can say I have these qualities in a measure, some, sadly, in a very *small* measure! And *you*?

I still fall short on occasion when under pressure. For example, I'm irritated when things don't go my way—I lose my peace. I don't always exercise self-control in a tense situation. I don't want to excuse such lapses by saying, "Well, I'm only human, no one is perfect!" I am constantly challenged by Scripture to aim high, and not settle for "nobody's perfect," and so remain where I am. Here's why: In the Letter to the Hebrews we are told to "follow after, or pursue, holiness. . ." to pursue something, involves intention, it involves purpose.

I am intentional in seeking to be a holy man for my Savior's purpose. I do not accept that, having come as far as I have, that I've come far enough. In Philippians we are exhorted to become "blameless and harmless, children of God without fault in the midst of a crooked and perverse generation, among whom you shine as *lights* in the world." I want to measure up to that description of a disciple, don't you? Blameless, and harmless, without fault. I want to have a testimony like that of Daniel.

QUITE A TESTIMONY

He was, you will remember, in Babylon—pagan, ungodly Babylon. Working in that unspiritual environment, Daniel—diligent and faithful to the true God—got promotion after promotion in his sphere of employment. This angered his colleagues, so they set about trying to "dig up dirt" about him. You can be sure of this, they must have been very thorough in their investigation of his conduct and his work record! "But," we read, "They could find *no* charge or fault, because *he was faithful!*" (Daniel 6:4)

Now notice *their* testimony of Daniel, "We shall not find *any* charge against this Daniel, unless we find it against him concerning the Law of his God." (Daniel 6:5) Wouldn't you be pleased to hear friends say that about you? I know I would. It was not his friends who said this. These were his detractors, his enemies! Indeed, Daniel qualified as being "blameless and harmless," a true light for the Lord in a dark world, prefiguring the church of Jesus Christ that was to be born through His death and resurrection. I want a testimony like that, don't you? How can I hope to become more Christlike than I am now? Answer: We must not settle for the status quo. I haven't come "far enough," and, I'll bet, neither have you! Paul writes, "I have not already attained. . ." The great apostle! His aspiration challenges us, "I press on . . . that I may *lay hold* of that for which Christ Jesus has also laid hold of me." "I press on . . . I lay hold. . ." That expresses a passionate aspiration for more, don't you agree?

This verse in 2 Corinthians 3:18 helps me in my quest. "We all . . . beholding as in a mirror the glory of the Lord, are being transformed into the same image from glory to glory, as by the Spirit of the Lord." Simply put, be intentional, press on, look to Jesus, seek His Face by consistent prayer. Be Christ-centered, not Self-centered, and the Holy Spirit does the work of transforming us. Isn't that grace? In fact, its *Surprising Grace*!

I'm thinking now of the words of a chorus we used to sing way back in the 60's when I did the music for the Assembly in my hometown. Here they are:

"Let the beauty of Jesus be seen in me,
All His wondrous compassion and purity.
O, Thou Spirit Divine, all my nature refine,
Til the beauty of Jesus be seen in me."

Amen Lord! That expresses my supreme aspiration. Won't you make it yours? Along with my aspirations, I also have some. . .

CONCERNS

The main one:
- The diminishing of the authority of the Bible in the lives of Christians.

This is not necessarily widespread among professing Christians. But, it *is* noticeable. A while ago, when talking to a lady, a church member, about Israel and the Palestinian issue, I quoted a verse which showed that the land belonged to Abraham's descendants, through Isaac and Jacob, not through Ishmael. She came back strongly, "Let's put aside the Bible. This is a racial issue!" Lay aside the Bible, in any dispute? Especially, in one so serious as the Middle East crisis? Though it's not widespread, as I've already observed, every now and then I blink, when I hear believers offer their own views on issues, without reference to what the Bible says about the subject, and in some cases their views are contrary to what it says! That doesn't seem to bother them!

ILLUSTRATING THE TREND

Let me lay out a few hypothetical instances of this trend, they summarize some encounters I have had in which believers show little or no regard for what the Scriptures teach, if the teachings cut across their preferences. A young fellow tells us he is in love with a nice young woman. He hopes to marry her. "Is she a Christian?" I ask. "No" he replies. "She is quite happy for me to go to church, and she even comes with me sometimes. I'm trusting God, He will save her." I point out the passage that warns, "Do not be unequally yoked together with unbelievers." He says, "But God loves her, and He will save her. We must just have faith!" They married, and divorced after just one year of marriage. You see, it's no good talking about faith, if we are in willful disobedience, going against the clear teaching of Scripture.

A Christian couple, both members of a church, decide to divorce. I counsel them, "God hates divorce, the Bible says. Why not back off from each other, give it some time, receive Bible counseling and trust God to heal the marriage, rather than break your vows?" The reply: "I don't think God wants us to stay together if we're so unhappy. So, thanks, but no thanks, we're getting divorced!"

A fine young Christian fellow, quite active in his church, says something like this "We can't make such a fuss about homosexuality, it's not the only sin. What about adultery, what about lying, stealing, and greed? To single out homosexuality seems pharisaical." True, it's not the only sin, these others mentioned are serious sins. However, homosexuality violates God's creation order of human sexuality, it confuses the sexual roles. It is written: "He made them *male* and *male*." Thus, men having sex with men, and women with women, is termed "an abomination, a detestable thing." The Gospel is God's power for salvation to everyone who believes, and that includes homosexuals. To diminish the seriousness of the sin, will not increase the likelihood of resulting in a desire for the Lord to change the person. This goes for all other sins as well.

This trend away from Biblical authority by professing believers, was brought sharply into focus by a United States President, himself a professing Christian, on a TV interview I watched. The interviewer said: "You are a Christian, and you support same-sex marriage. You are aware that many Christians believe that the Bible speaks against the practice of homosexuality?" His answer: "We cannot take an *obscure passage* in Romans to speak against same sex relationships." The President said more, but I was thinking, that's astonishing! Parts of Romans are "obscure passages?" Who decides which portions are obscure?

Then we have a popular Christian minister who, in a recent book declares that there is no hell, and no eternal punishment. This, in spite of the numerous references to both hell and eternal judgment in the Scriptures, Jesus being the main proponent of this teaching! My concern is this: If we do not accept the Scriptures as our authority for all matters of life, and if we do not walk by the light of the Word, then we have to make a light for ourselves, and that is *scary*!

DANGER

See what the Lord says about this "make your own light" practice: "Watch out, you who live in your own light and warm yourselves by your own fires. This is the reward you will receive from Me: you will soon lie down in great torment." (Isaiah 50:11 NLT)

We want to rather emulate the Psalmist who writes. "Your Word is a lamp to my feet and a light to my path." Do you want to have God's special attention? Then take heed to Isaiah 66:2. ". . .to this one I will look: he who is humble and contrite of spirit and who trembles at My Word." (NASB) We need to exhibit a healthy fear of the Lord—which is the beginning of wisdom, and this is manifested by our regard for, and obedience to, the Bible. In every situation, every crisis, every controversy, let us firstly ask: "What does the Bible say?" and then seek to apply its principles to the situation. Let's love the Word, like Jeremiah, who said, "Your Words were found and I ate them, and Your Word was to me the joy and rejoicing of my heart, for I am called by Your Name." While in this "not yet" stage of my life, I also cherish certain. . .

DELIGHTS

These are some of the things that give me great pleasure, they are enjoyment triggers off great thankfulness to the Lord, "who gives us richly all things to enjoy."

Our backyard birds, we are fortunate in that our backyard is bounded on three sides by a forest of very tall trees, some of these extend as high as a four or five-storey building. In the clearing where our bird feeders hang, we enjoy a visual feast of feathered creatures, ranging from the tiny ones—sparrows, finches, nuthatches, titmouses, and the even tinier chickadees—to the larger varieties, which include woodpeckers, bluejays, doves, and the spectacularly colourful red cardinals. We also attract a veritable army of pigeons, beautiful birds, but they can send the birdseed bill "up on high," so they are not so welcome. We have to use bird feeders that they cannot easily access, in order to avoid going bankrupt! Same with the squirrels. But, that's a different matter! When I see them, I want to ask Brother Noah why he took a pair of those pests on board the Ark! They are destructive and diabolically clever—after a while, they manage to find a way to "crack" even the most "squirrel-proof" feeder, in order to steal some of the birdseed! However, of late we have been able to deal with them a little more effectively.

Canoeing on the Mohawk River also affords me great pleasure. At several of the launching places in our area, the river is broad, and bounded on either side by tall forests. It's a great delight for me to paddle my own canoe for a while and enjoy the tranquility of the waterway. Beats a motor-driven craft any day!

I also enjoy cycling on the bike path. One can go for miles along these specially designated, paved paths, which mostly parallel the river. It's good exercise, and gives me cause to praise God, both for the scenery and for the ability, at my age, to still actively enjoy the beauty of His creation. Beats golfing any day! (I've always considered golfing just a good walk, spoiled!)

Another source of delight is my involvement in the Radio ministry. It affords me great pleasure to complete the scripts for my Radio talks, and to record them for broadcast. I am blessed to be on one Radio station twice a day, seven days a week, and on another, once every day, Monday thru Friday. What a privilege to be able to construct a message, time it to perfection (within seconds) for broadcast, and know that the Word of the Lord is going out to thousands of listeners. Of course, we know not everyone is listening attentively to the message. The seed is being sown (broadcast) and we do have a fairly steady trickle of folk coming to the church, because they say they first heard about us on the Radio. These short talks are also aired over Trans World Radio in Malawi, and on CCFM in Cape Town. As Julie Andrews sings in "Sound of Music," these are a few of my favorite things. They provide me with much delight, for which I thank the Lord.

1st PRIZE

But, what gives me the greatest pleasure is this. Knowing that people to whom we have ministered over the years, are *going on* with the Lord. I think I can understand Paul's feelings about the Thessalonian believers. Being parted from them, he worried about their spiritual state, particularly because they were experiencing persecution for their faith. On receiving Timothy's good report about their spiritual condition, the relieved apostle wrote, "Now we live, if you stand fast in the Lord." (1 Thessalonian 3:8)

Merle and I have no greater delight than to hear that folk who have sat under our ministry over the years, are going on with the Lord, some, in full-time ministry, others shining as lights in their job situation and in their local community. As the apostle stated: "What is our hope, or joy, or crown of rejoicing? Is it not even you in the presence of our Lord Jesus Christ at His coming?" (1 Thessalonian 2:19)

You see, all we will have to present to the Lord on that day will be *people*—folk who have come to faith in Him and who have grown spiritually, at least in part, through our ministry. What delight this gives me! "*You* are our hope, our joy, our crown of rejoicing!" All because, in His surprising grace— He has used us to point you to Him and to help build you up in your faith. I say "surprising grace," because we are—in human terms—extremely unlikely candidates for this role.

Early on, as I was starting out in the ministry, the Lord gave me three passages of Scripture, which I knew were specifically His Word to me. All through the 40-something years of my ministry, these verses have stayed with me, strengthening and guiding me. I call them my "life verses."

(Philippians 1:6) "Being confident of this very thing, that He who has begun a good work in you will complete it until the day of Jesus Christ." When this word came to me, I was really struggling with temptations, living in defeat. I wondered if I was going to make it as a Christ follower. The realization that the Lord who had begun a work in me was not going to quit and give up on me, lifted me out of my discouragement and uncertainty, and infused me with a God-dependency that has carried me through many tests and trials, since then.

(1 Chronicles 22:18[a]-19) "Is not the Lord your God with you? Now set your heart and your soul to seek the Lord your God. Therefore, arise and *build*..." This word gave me direction for my ministry. From the beginning, I have always sought to build the Word of God steadily and systematically into people's lives, avoiding the temptation to attract people by novelties and gimmicks. One can gather a whole lot of bricks quite easily, but one needs to *build* something with the bricks, and that's a process, not a wham-bam, spectacular event. That's how I see the work of God. Paul wrote: "Let every man take heed *how* he builds." Because, he said, our work for the

Lord will be tested by fire on that day. I don't want my "building" the fruit of my ministry to be burned up on that day. Thus, for every plan and strategy, I always ask, what are we building? Will it last, will it survive the fire?

(2 Chronicles 16:9[a]) "For the eyes of the Lord run to and fro throughout the whole earth, to show Himself strong on behalf of those whose heart is loyal to Him."

Whenever I have to face a daunting task, I remember. He has promised to act with strength on my behalf, as long as my heart is completely His. There have been many times when I have felt intimidated by some situation I have had to deal with. At such times I have prayed, "Lord, I'm not equal to this task. You know my heart, I am completely Yours. So, please HELP!" and He always comes through for me strongly, as He promised!

CONCLUSION—THE BOOK— NOT MY LIFE— AT LEAST, NOT YET!

The grace of God that saved me all of 50 years ago still surprises me, guiding me, upholding me and enabling me to serve Him despite my inadequacies, which are many! If this account of His grace activities in my life has stirred you to reach up and lay hold of His strong hand, and if you have been inspired to say like Caleb said: "Now, give me this mountain," whatever challenge "this mountain" represents for you, then I will consider it a great privilege to have been a testimony to the Lord's

SURPRISING

GRACE!!

ERRATA

Page 58:
  "Stategy" should read
  "Strategy"

CPSIA information can be obtained at www.ICGtesting.com
Printed in the USA
BVOW071234100512

289845BV00002B/2/P